# Sex,

# Dating and

# REALLY Confusing

# Girls!

*By*

# Sue Ostler

Published in the UK by MX Publishing, 335 Princess Park Manor, Royal Drive, London, N11 3GX

www.mxpublishing.co.uk

Cover Design by Staunch Design

www.staunch.com

# Lust In Translation

Feisty, flirty and effortlessly funny, Sue Ostler is the author of five books on the subject of all things mating, dating and matchmaking.

Known as the Flirt Diva, and hailed as the Queen of Love, Sue's signature book <u>Flirt Diva</u> was aimed at single, sassy women who wanted to learn to flirt. Encouraged by those same women who said, *'But what about the men?'* she sat down and compiled her knowledge into an instructional manual for men.

Sue has entertained the troops across London's single's scene with hundreds of events, from the West End's infamous Flirt Schmooze & Shimmies to Hen's Parties, Men-Only masterclasses, oh, and the occasional stand-up comedy gig, since she arrived from Sydney on the day of the London bombings in 2005 – talk about an explosive welcome!

Thanks to her books, columns, live events and appearances across the world's leading media – Sue has helped clients worldwide and has the heart-warming testimonials to show for it.

Sue's undying belief that there's a Flirt Superstar in every man, woman and hormonally challenged teen, has developed into a unique career, and a nomination as Australian Woman of the Year in the UK 2010 and 2011.

# Warning!

In order to attract a beyootiful woman you need to push yourself and take risks. You must have the enthusiasm and bravado of an SAS lieutenant, and be prepared to drop your stiff upper lip. You should be willing to face the good, the bad and the ugly, and take a deep breath and say, *WTF!* Above all you have to be resilient and persistent because, as my good friend's Uncle Tony says, *"It's a numbers game."* And it can be tough. But don't worry. It's all part of the fun. So long as you're aware that at some point, you will screw up.

That's where I come into it. As a dating expert, it's my job to take you out of your comfort zone and hassle you about hedonistic-supercharged-sexual-flexibility – oh, and dating related issues. Consequently this book will make you want to meet women and go on dates – and much more.

When involved in active dating, you will need to keep your intensity under control. Avoid gestures which involve quick, sudden moves in any direction. Make sure you're not sweating as this is a sign that your body is overheating; keeping well hydrated helps to avoid this. I also advise wearing a heart-rate monitor and keeping an eye on it throughout. Don't worry about being embarrassed though, since studies show that people are more trusting of people who are easily embarrassed, so you can go as red in the face as you like – especially in those situations where it can't be avoided, like in the face of show-stopping, jaw-dropping beauty.

Dating and seduction can seriously affect your ability to concentrate as well. The inability to concentrate could reduce the success of the forthcoming challenges. Therefore you will need some tips on how to manage it, and what to expect. Rest assured there will be moments where you feel the pain, and moments when you cringe. I've anticipated those, so I'm going to nip them in the bud by saying – deal with it! Keep your eye on the ball and by the time you get to the end, you'll be able to spot a babe with trouble on her mind at twenty paces.

5

**Author's Disclaimer**

The following contains elements of humour and serious commentary. The reader is advised that no warnings are made as to the elements intended as humour, or those intended as serious commentary. Failure on the part of the reader to detect discernable differences between humorous and serious passages and/or elements shall not be deemed a defect in this book for legal purposes. Nor shall such failure be deemed to imply a defect in the reader.

Frequent references are made throughout to Englishmen and women – this refers not only to those who were born on this great island, but those who have lived here long enough to be an integral part of British society.

Lastly, the names and details of all people and places have been changed to protect the innocent.

To access more Secret Women's Information, email: sue@flirtdiva.com.

*This book is dedicated to the best boyfriend in Britain.*

*I love you very much.*

## Step 1. Walking the Walk       Pg 16

1. *Why Is It So Hard To Approach Women?*

2. *It started As A Social Experiment*

3. *Real Men Do Flirt!*

4. *Internationally Recognized Flirting Gestures*

5. *Body Language Maths*

6. *Eye-Contact*

7. *Spot the Flirt*

8. *What Signals Should YOU Be On The Look-Out For?*

9. *What Signals is SHE On The Look Out For?*

10. *Rrrrjection*

11. *What Women Want*

12. *New Kid on the Kop*


## Step 2. Talking the Talk       Pg 72

1. *It's Not the Sausage, it's the Sizzle*

2. *Don't Get Mad, Get Funny!*

3. *Sorry, What Did You Say...?*

4. *Compliment-itis*

5. *Questions, Ice-Breakers and Random Openers*

6. *They Say That Listening Is The Sexiest...*

7. *Dodgy Pick-up Lines*

8. *What Women Want*

9. *New Kid on the Kop*

### Step 3. Looking & Living The Part     Pg 126

1. *Hey Good Lookin'*
2. *Style Guru*
3. *If you look good, you can get away with anything!*
4. *Let's Get Physical*
5. *I Need a Hero!*
6. *Boys Night In*
7. *Sizzling & Saucy Seductresses*
8. *What Women Want*
9. *New Kid on the Kop*

### Step 4. Building Your Dating Profile     Pg 176

1. *Psycho-Sexual Admin*
2. *Romance Resume*
3. *The C Word: Topping up your Confidence*
4. *Alpha Dog Vs the Shy Guy*
5. *What Makes You A Good Catch?*
6. *Mind Candy*
7. *Baggage*
8. *Fancy a Type?*
9. *Wing-women & Chemistry*
10. *The Friend Zone*
11. *What Women Want*
12. *New Kid on the Kop*

## Step 5. You got to fight for your right to PAAARTTY!    Pg 220

1.  *Action Man*

2.  *And Your Speciality Is….*

3.  *Bachelor Pad*

4.  *Gonzo Travel Dude*

5.  *From Workaholic to Weekend Warrior*

6.  *What Women Want*

7.  *New Kid on the Kop*


## Step 6. Now You Do It!    Pg 254

1.  *Hanky-Panky Happy Hour*

2.  *Hit List*

3.  *Booze, Online Dating….And Sex*

4.  *Booze, Organised Dating…And Sex*

5.  *Real World Socialising*

6.  *Location, Location, Location*

7.  *How's Your Approach?*

8.  *Closing the Deal*

9.  *She's Not That Into You*

10. *What Women Want*

11. *New Kid on the Kop*

# What Makes Me The Big Expert?

I wrote my first dating advice book in 1998. It helped me deal with the break-up from hell. I figured that turning to writing as heartbreak therapy was better than drowning in a life of vodka soaked misery. I've been studying this dating lark ever since. And I've had a hoot. What is it they say? Don't get mad, get even. Needless to say I never looked back. And somehow I stumbled across the love of my life along the way. *Jackpot!*

I moved to London in 2005 to develop my studies. I've been at the frontline studying girls and boys at play ever since. As part of my worldwide Flirt Diva Discovery tour, I've spent the past few years trawling bars, clubs, pubs, cafes, singles halls, speed-dating events and meat markets up and down the land to see people in action and get them to sample my approach to flirting.

And I'm not just watching; I'm interacting. As a woman who's travelled mainly solo around the UK, from naughty Newcastle – the pulling capital, to good-time Glasgow and everywhere in-between, I've been hit on enough times to know what works and what doesn't. These days I'm offended if I *don't* get hit on! So hey, I've got a lot to say on the subject.

My motivation is simple, there are close to twenty-million single adults in Britain, and I'll be damned if I can't get those numbers down. Or at the very worst, set you on the right path to get yourself a crafty smooch. *We need more sex please, we're British!*

In October 2010 I hosted a singles event with *Time Out* magazine. Along with the general shenanigans, we created an award for the best flirt. A chap in his late twenties arrived midway through the party. He introduced himself, a stocky fellow, pleasant enough looking, but no George Clooney. I had my hands full with a particularly difficult blonde, a real drama queen. I nodded towards three attractive women huddled in the corner and said. *"Go and talk to them!"* I didn't see him again until much later. There he was, chatting and laughing – thoroughly entertaining them. *'Well done!'*

I mouthed as I threw him a wink. An hour or so later he told me he'd secured two phone numbers. I was impressed and told him so. *Who knew?*

Next thing he'd dashed off to chat up another lady. Pretty soon they were bumping and grinding and minutes later, they were snogging their hearts out! My mouth just fell open. It was that time of night where everyone had their beer goggles on, but even so...! Shortly after, I presented him with the Best Flirt Award – of course I did! *Cue cheering and whooping please!*

Two weeks later he came to collect his prize, a face-to-face consultation with moi. We met at a Soho bar and settled in with beers and Bellinis. He filled me in on what had happened since we last met. He was actively dating one of the girls from the party. He'd also met a second girl he was rather smitten with, and to cap it off, he'd struck up a thing with a third young lady. His dilemma, and the advice he sought from me, was whether it was morally ethical to date the three women simultaneously.

I sat open mouthed. This was a guy who'd been through a two-year dating drought – he was top of the flops, no doubt about it. Yet from the moment he entered that party, it was all systems go. He'd gone from zero to hero in the space of a two short weeks.

Frank Spencer meets Errol Flynn!

The sole reason from his point of view, was the massive confidence boost he'd got from approaching the trio of hot babes at the party. He jumped in the deep end and swam for his life. Unless I'd specifically sent him on the 'three woman mission', he never would have found the courage to approach. Once he had a taste, he wanted more. My heart swelled with pride.

It's precisely because of these experiences, along with the awe-inspiring feedback I've had from my weekly male masterclasses, that I've shifted my focus to men. It just made sense. Right from the beginning when I started coaching women, we typically ended up talking about the men's role in all this. The woman would get all feisty and ask: *"Why are you telling us? Why aren't you telling the men as well?"* *"Jolly japes"*. I thought. *"Of course!"*

Now I'm set to share all my Secret Women's Information because what's the point of women having all the knowledge? What you'll find here is a female point of view on all the topics that I get asked about the most. You'll also find a plan, a strategy and a billion ways to get to first base.

*Now it's over to you...*

# Step 1. Walking the Walk

## Why Is It So Hard To Approach Women?

I've spoken with all kinds of women the world over, from the weak and weary, loud and lairy, hot and hairy, and believe you me, when it comes to the women of Britain, every last one of them agrees on one thing, they're not getting hit on. Or if they are, it's by the WRONG kind of guy: the players, the cocky twats, the all-sizzle-no-steak guys we don't take seriously. It's not by the quality blokes. It's not by the keepers. It's not by YOU! And that my friend, is the reason they're single.

But it's not the only reason. Britain has a singles phenomenon on its hands and it's easy to see why. Men are expected to make all the moves but they're not. That's because women aren't giving out the green light signals. As a result blokes are dazed and confused and rooted to the spot. We're at a stalemate. Everyone's lost the plot and it's all based on a big, fat misunderstanding because women, bless them, have a knack of looking terrifically sassy on the surface, but burrow down a little, and they're wobblier than Nigella Lawon's sherry trifle when it comes to this love stuff.

Is it just a storm in a British teacup? Hell no! It's a key theme. I see it firsthand every Friday night. That's because I have a job where I pilot a gaggle of girls out on a flirting foray across Central London. The Flirt Schmooze & Shimmy is a lot of things, but mainly it's a booze fuelled laugh. Women of all ages come along to build up their confidence and get out of their comfort zone. We visit bars and clubs, from the super swanky to the downright cheesy and the girls do challenges to help get them over the hump.

Over the years I've seen all types of girls, and experienced every possible scenario. I've witnessed plenty of psycho-sexual victories and just as many car-crashes. I've seen the effects of the leg-quivering fear of rejection, and the heart wrenching criticism that these flirty and feisty girls unfurl on themselves. I've been there at the front-line, watching all the action. So don't tell me it's tough out there, I bloody well know it is!

16

Week in, week out I hear the same things over and over again. And frankly it's stuff you should know; stuff you need to know. Moreover since you're probably not privy to this kind of thing, I'm sharing it here. Am I talking out of school? Maybe. But tough! 'Cos I'm on your side.[1]

The biggest challenge for women in the dating arena is that they *lack both the confidence and the skills* to let on that they fancy you. It's not that they don't *want* to flirt. Hell no. Half the time they don't even know *how* to flirt! It's not their fault. It's just not their thing. Just because they're women doesn't mean it comes naturally.

There are a million and one reasons why – psychological, physiological and traditional, but drill down and in all likelihood it's simply because they've not grown up in touchy-feely, lovey-dovey households where everyone went around having soppy group hugs. As a nation it's just not something we do. The harsh British climate doesn't help either. It's not like boys and girls grew up flirting and frolicking half naked on the beach as the hormonally charged teen spirit kicked in. Instead everyone was huddled around the telly keeping a stiff upper lip. This is not a criticism, nor it is it a personal weakness, it's a British thing. And according to the ladies I coach, it can make things tricky if you're looking to meet someone.

---

[1] *All names and locations have been changed.*

## What Single Women Are REALLY Saying...

*"I am the world's most impossible flirt! I cannot flirt to save myself. If I like a guy I ignore him! I need to make the right kind of connection but I don't know how."* Katy 26

*"I'm in my mid-twenties and can't flirt to save my life. I am quite sarcastic, wouldn't dare chat up a man, and men hardly approach me, because I'm unapproachable. Don't get me wrong, I am friendly, outgoing and funny 'supposedly"*...Jo 29

*"I don't know how to flirt for fear of coming across either arrogant or ridiculous".* Caitlin 32

*"I'm a confident, independent, happy singleton... who just can't seem to flirt!"* Shana 34

*"I don't know why but I ALWAYS say the wrong things..."* Alex 39

*"I cannot even look someone in the eye! Help!"* Jackie 36

*"I am absolutely hopeless when it comes to flirting....I completely ignore the blokes I like!"* Jody 27

*"I have absolutely no idea of flirting and am seriously in need of finding out about it."* Becca 31

*"Am hopeless at pulling men (walking past the ones I fancy a hundred times & looking at them when they are not looking at me as heaven forbid I should make eye contact!)"* Lisa 29

On top of dealing with their own shortcoming and insecurities, women are also saying that blokes need to make more of an effort – they need to *"hit on us more"*. But for the most part, it's not happening. It's not the done thing. And I for one am not surprised. Nobody in this country makes eye-contact or heaven forbid speak to a stranger, let alone asks anyone on a date! Well OK, that's not true everywhere, particularly not up North where people literally fall over themselves to be friendly, but certainly if you live in big old busy London then hello – tough city! [2]

A friend explained it thus: *"Look, if someone's sat alone in a café, that makes it easier to approach; but if you're at a bar or a pub, women don't sit alone; so if I'm in a bar and I see a hot girl sat over there with her mates, I'm not going to go over and start chatting. It's not going to happen. It feels too weird. I'm putting myself on the line. If it doesn't go well, I've got to live with that."*

OK, point taken, but if that's your take on it, then Houston, we've got a problem. Hear me out here…by not going out on a limb to meet new people you're effectively eliminating a massive portion of the population. And once you do away with meeting new women 'cold' – how on earth are you meant to you meet them? Oh sure you might stumble across them through friends of friends, or in the workplace, but that comes with its own set of complications – you know what they say, don't screw the crew!

The trick when it comes to topping up your social circle is to widen your options, take the risks and increase your chances. Remember what my good friend's Uncle Tony said: *"It's a numbers game."* You've got to fight for your right to party – or at the very least, think more broadly.

---

[2] *Speaking personally it was a big culture shock when I first arrived in London. I didn't realize it was illegal to talk to strangers, especially not on the tube! Guess who learnt the hard way? Fortunately it's not so bad outside of London.*

Let's get to the guts of the matter, why is it so damn hard to approach women? Is it because they struggle to show their availability? And if so why? Is it because it makes them feel 'desperate' so they come across as cool, or some might say haughty, acting like they don't have to lift a goddam finger. And if that is indeed the case, then of course you're not going to make any moves because you are not getting the signals. It's the classic Catch 22, Action-Reaction scenario. We've got all the gear, but no idea!

Simply put, British women, well most women for that matter, are caught in a historical time-warp when it comes to all things romance. They may command equality in the boardroom, the bedroom and in the financial stakes, but put them in front of a cute guy and they would rather eat their own wedding finger than show they fancy you, or, heaven forbid, make the first move.

Then big question is: *"How are you supposed to tell if she fancies you?"* In a perfect world the answer would be simple. *She does that thing girls do...* She grins at you and does the touchy-feelies: a light pat here, a playful pinch there. She looks into your eyes and flicks her hair; she touches your arm, your shoulder, your thigh…She smothers you in big boozy hugs and flashes her knickers and knockers. *Why, she practically straddles you.* Except that she doesn't.

OF COURSE she doesn't!

*What the fudge?* Why not?

Because in Britain the vast majority of women do not flirt like sex-crazed demons. Englishwomen may be good at a lot of things, but overt flirting is not one of them. They pull a blank when it comes to, you know, signalling their availability. We're talking the basics: smiling, eye-contact – anything to let on that they fancy you! It's the story of great British misadventure. What can I say?

The other worrying thing is that even if she flirted with you like mad, most of you wouldn't recognise a green light signal if it jumped up and hit you on the nose. Admit it!! And that oversight can cost you dearly. One of my girlfriends put into plain words the reason she gave up on the guy she was flirting with: *"He kept looking over, but he wouldn't do anything about it."* Case in point! But don't feel bad about it. It's no-one's fault. We may be a lot of things; but a nation of flirts we are not. Frankly we're more interested in other things. *Beer and pizza comes to mind.*

Of course it would be easier if the ladies were to make themselves **more visibly available for dating.** But how could they do that? By wearing Hi-Vis jackets in lime and orange stripes? Assuming they don't fancy that idea, what else can they do? Oh wait, here's an idea, they could be all flirty and dish out all the obvious signs, that way you'll know they're keen and you'll be able to make a move with complete confidence. *What a great idea 'eh?* Yes and you'll be waiting for hell to freeze over before it happens.

I'm not saying that British women are prudes, far from it. Once they get warmed up, they're absolutely fine. Especially when they're out on the town and they're completely bongoed. The problem is their tendency to clam up and turn to jelly when they spot someone they sodding well fancy.

But believe you me, if I could change one thing; it would be to wave my magic wand and *Abracadabra…*All the Single Ladies… *all the single ladies*/Would put their hands up…*put your hands up!* They'd be all flirty and perky, and a wee bit dirty and they'd swish their hair and do all those girly things that even YOU recognise as flirting, if for no other reason than you've seen it done to perfection from the floozies in the movies. You would respond by striding boldly over, dipping your cap and saying, *"Why m'lady, your delicious brazenness makes me blush!"* Then you pin her arms to her side and kiss her – long, hard kisses.

Because whether you're a down-to-earth guy, a shy guy, a geekie guy, or a larger than life guy – there's some sweet, gorgeous girl out there that would like to get to know you…but first she's got meet you! Someone's got to make a move – and that someone is you. And until you get that into your thick skull, then gentlemen of Great Britain – we have a problem!

So how did things get to this point and how can we change them?

Well for starters next time you're out having a pint and you notice an *all-smiling-all-flirting female,* you've simply got to take action and make a move. So if you look over yonder and lock eyes and your heart starts hammering and you think she's flirting with you, you've *got* to give her the benefit of the doubt.

### *Picture this:*

You spot her. She smiles and makes eyes at you.

You argue furiously with yourself.

*Is she flirting? No surely she's not flirting.*

Oh yes she is. *She's flirting!*

You wander over to introduce yourself and say something funny.

She laughs so hard that everyone in the bar looks and stares.

She cocks her head and looks up at you hopefully.

You draw her towards you and kiss her cheek and then step away.

She pulls you back and looks you dead in the eye.

*She's not nervous or giggly or fidgety – she just wants you to kiss her damn it!*

And there you are – half naked in a strange woman's flat.

*Shazam!*

Of course this will never happen if you're too scared to make a move, or too cool for school. It's only the very brave who get the girl. And once you're in with a chance, you've got to have your wits about you. Rather than freezing on the spot, you've got to figure out how to cop off with her – and that takes practice!

So if you're a guy who doesn't necessarily think your god's gift, but thinks you're, you know, alright; and you're not necessarily looking for Miss World but you're looking for a great girl, someone funny, sweet and quirky with all the trimmings and special features, along with a heartfelt experience that will right the wrongs of the human race and place the axis of the world back on its rightful axis, then we need to get this party started! And that means:

✓ *You need to lose the heebie-jeebies*

✓ *In order to lose the heebie-jeebies, you need to go out and practice*

✓ *In order to practice, you need to lose your fear of rejection*

✓ *In order to lose your fear of rejection, you need to low-risk situations*

✗ *NOT high-risk situations with the love of your life!*

✓ *Then approach confidently, without any tricks or gimmicks.*

***Thought For The Day:*** *You may completely miss that she's flirting with you but from HER point of view, she's R-E-A-L-L-Y putting it out there. Why she's being so brazen she could bust. Even Blind Freddy can see what's going on! But, you're not Blind Freddy – you're just a dumb guy, no offense – and you don't get it. And fair enough, because if she were any more subtle, she would have her head up her own...oh never mind!*

## Some Background About Our Dating Culture…

You could say the British dating model is pretty casual, and you would be right. Everything happens by chance. Our idea of a good time is to go out for a drink with friends and meet a friend of a friend, preferably someone we fancy. We have a laugh and a drink and a few more drinks; share a drunken kiss, grab a kebab and go home and shag. We wake up in the morning and say: *'Erm, this is a bit awkward.'* And then we carry on.

In other words we don't live in a flirting culture, unlike say New York. A place where the gung-ho take-no-prisoners approach to dating explodes in a relentless, riotous frenzy of flirting – and much more. The advantage is that we don't get dragged down in the rigorous rituals and frankly mind bogglingly complicated multi-dating concepts of our US counterparts. Nor do English lads have the cocky jock-schlock of the US dudes who exude outrageous swagger and confidence; or for that matter the Italians who have a tendency to overdo the charm to the point of being utterly laughable. And we're certainly not like the French – but they're overrated anyway. *Oui!*

The Brits are an entity unto their own when it comes to personal expression, utterly charming and sometimes rather naughty but not naughty enough. Well the saying *'No sex please we're British'* had to come from somewhere didn't it? It's no secret that the Brits are polite and reserved – lovely on a good day and ever so passively aggravating on a bad day. So we like waiting in queues – hey, nothing wrong with that!

When it comes to the women, rather than taunting and flaunting her sexuality and playing with your mind, body and soul, your British beauty is likely to make her feelings about as clear as ah, mud. Unlike other nationalities who at the risk of disposable stereotyping, will let you know exactly where you stand. Picture those red-hot Spanish babes and the Italian firecrackers, and of course the sexy Scandinavians, and at a pinch the Antipodeans. And who could forget the jaw-dropping eroticism of Eastern

European and Oriental women and the bolshy New Yawk gals? When these ladies flirt with you, you'll know about it all right.

But when it comes to your English lass, it's slightly more pedestrian. Of course there are always exceptions but generally speaking, she's likely to smile a bit, fidget and maybe play with her hair. She might even puff her chest out and bat her eyes at you, and if you're very lucky, remove a speck of fluff from halfway up your bare arm. From there, you're supposed to gauge that she's hot for you. Tricky business when you don't have a clue what's going on! Not that it's your fault mind; it's just that she's in the midst of a nervous breakdown.

Thanks to paranoia to the left of her and insecurities to the right along with the all-consuming-terror of coming across as *DESPERATE*, she reins it in and tones it down to the point that – blink and you miss it. Fine for her, she's just preserving her dignity. Not so good for you unless you have titanic-bionic superpowers. Otherwise you'll never get that she fancies you in a million years.

Don't get me wrong, women don't play-hard-to-get intentionally and they don't do it to be difficult. They do it because, just like you, they are utterly, painfully, gobsmackingly terrified of rejection. Even if she's bubbling over with more attitude than J-Lo's butt on the surface, underneath, she feels sillier than Alice in Blunderland: shy, scared and psychotic.

Fun Fact: *Our ability to flirt has a lot to do with our culture. I'm from Australia – an extremely flirt friendly place, partly due to the warm environment and the sunny disposition of the Aussies. Whenever I visit my hometown of Sydney I'm struck by how crazy it is down there on Oxford St on a Saturday night. Everyone's freakishly tall, tanned, toned with dresses up to here and shoes this high. And that's just the blokes! But I'll tell you one thing they know how to flirt. They will check you out and give you the once over and remind you that you're a woman. Who cares if they're trannies! Hey we take our flirting where we can get it!*

25

### You're Not The Messiah, Just A Very Naughty Boy

Getting across that you fancy someone is a two way street. The key thing is to learn how to read the signals and watch like a hawk. Then you need to send a few of your own which can be easier said than done, since within the world of Internationally Recognised Flirting Gestures, women have around 556 ways to show their attraction.

*Men have about 3!*

So you could say that women have the upper hand when it comes to signalling their interest – if they choose to that is. From their ability to drop sex bombs via lustful bedroom eyes and sexy hip-thrusts, to the touch-feelies, they've got the power to flirt up a storm. Yet they hold back. With the end result that both sexes fail to connect when it comes to transmitting sensory messages via the erotic system of sign language. *What is it* that makes us so hopeless?

*Here's how it currently looks:*

➢ Boy spots Girl

➢ Girl declines to send the signals, or 'drop her White Hanky' as it were

➢ Boy fails to approach because there's no signal – no Green Light

➢ Boy and Girl miss out on the Love Of Their Life because they're both too stubborn, or too scared, to do anything about it

  *So much for the Happy Ending!*

Bottom line, if you don't approach her, it's never going to happen!

  *This is terrible!*

And it's the reason I embarked on this project.

## It Started As A Social Experiment...

I wanted to know who the most confident and authentic men were. I wanted to know how they did it. I wanted to understand the issues when it comes to approaching women. I *needed* to know, so I could compile this, The Flirter's Guide to Great Britain and pass it on to the rest of you. I lured a bunch of chaps to the pub with the promise of a boozy night and free beers. After ordering the first round and unearthing a shared obsession with runaway sex, I started firing off questions:

*"What's hard about approaching women?"*

*"We can't find any decent girls to approach."* Said one fellow.

*"We can't find any girl, let alone a decent girl!"* Moaned another!

*"They only see me as a friend!"* Groaned the rest.

*"They just make rules up and don't tell us why,"* One shrugged.

*"How many new women are you meeting weekly - not from your immediate friend or work circle?"* I asked.

*"None!"* Came the overriding answer.

*"Less than one!"* said another.

Hmmmm...Well let me ask YOU: when was the last time you took a chance on having a random chat to someone you fancied? Have you tried a cold approach recently – or ever? Shame on you if you haven't, *Gah! Fury!*

This is the part where there are no excuses; you just have to be bold. Banish the idea that women don't like being approached. They don't mind being approached, so long as you're not a complete twat about it. The most important thing is *how* you approach. Make or break it – it's up to you. You'll be in with a chance if your approach is light, breezy – and not even remotely sleazy. Getting past hello is the hard part, but once you're over the hump it's easy. The only challenge is to have a laugh and not come on too strong. At the end of the day girls are just like you; they beat themselves up and feel nervous about everything from how to keep the banter going to how they look.

Word of warning: if you do make an approach, and the minx in question responds by, miracle of miracles, making her availability clear by dishing out the looks and hooks – and you want to end this night acting out things you've seen in porn movies – then you need to respond in a likeminded fashion. Fight flirt with flirt! Otherwise she will retreat back into her shell and that will be that. All ze sexy pozzibiliteez dead in ze water. So be very clear about one thing – snooze, you lose Mister.

*Bottom line: Once you get the Green Light, move quickly!*

As hard as it is, and as odd as it feels know that you *have to make an effort*. That's your role as a modern day super trooper. You have an important part to play in all this and you can't put it in the too hard basket. It takes two to tango and your role is vital. Don't underestimate it.

---

### The Bloke Quote

Author and general man-about-town Toby Young has this to say about the wiles of the Englishwoman: *"Judging by her body language, she was unmistakably British. She gave me an apologetic look as if to say I know this is awkward but what can I do? English women, they may not be celebrated for their innate sexual sense of style as French women are, but there is something deeply attractive about their natural diffidence. Evelyn Waugh said that charm is a quality that doesn't exist outside the British Isles' and that's particularly true of our women. the famous pin up girls of the 1950s and 60s Monroe, Bardot, Loren – all have an in your face raunchiness that isn't nearly as appealing as the quiet sex appeal of Sylvia Syms. Like her, Caroline had the knack of turning her embarrassment into a form of flirtation. A uniquely British trick. Here confidence and sense of self was all the more attractive for being understated."*

–The Times. May 2011.

# Real Men Do Flirt!

The goal here is to be bombastically successful with women – hot women, cool women and everything in-between. In order to be bombastically successful with women, you need to meet vast numbers of them, and you need to date. In order to date, you need to flirt. Most men don't rate flirting. They think it's a girl's game. Yet, the guy who flirts – is the guy who gets the girl.

*Let the flirting begin.*

If you want to morph into the Jedi Master of Flirting and show her what you're made of, you need to be on her wavelength. That means not revealing any stress or visible signs of distress: no lip-licking, sweating, heavy breathing or shaky hands. No rapid blinking, unseemly fidgeting or tensed shoulders. And don't overdo it – she doesn't want the Ringmaster of Cringe. She's looking for the C word: a man who's Confident.

There are three main components that make up this crazy little thing called flirting: **Body Language. Eye Contact** and **Banter.** Link them together with the Dating ABC's: **Approachable. Bulletproof. Confident** and you've got yourself a foolproof recipe for success. Make it your business to include these in your everyday life, and you will be unstoppable. Unstoppable I tell you.

Happily there are no hard and fast rules, in spite of what the textbooks say. So long as you're confident that you're broadcasting your message as clearly as possible, nature will do the rest and you'll be hooked, *and hooked up*, in no time at all. From here on in you can forget about being the worst single man in Britain, because the only question on everyone's lips will be, *"How can such a catch be single?"*

FORM AN ORDERLY QUEUE PLEASE LADIES!

Even if you are the world's most Unflirtwithable Man, think of it this way, flirting is a reminder you that you've got charm and you know how to use it. When used well, it's natural and playful – sleaze and cheese this is not. Nor is it a billion testosterone fuelled techniques – it's just *being yourself.* So I won't be asking you to pretend to be someone you're not anytime soon, but, I will be asking you to turn up the volume on your own personal style and make it flip right off the page.

The bonus with flirting is that it can't be one-sided. Well actually it can, but it's a bitch to keep flirting when you're doing it on your lonesome. If your playmate's not flirting back, you'll know about it soon enough and then, it's simply a matter of stepping away from the lady. It's no biggy. It's a learning curve. And in the process you may step on a few toes, but so what? You'll become more skilled over time. Soon you will possess the ability to mesmerise, sexualise and hold anyone completely in your power. And even if you do stumble, who cares? Just get back out there and give it another go.

And that's pretty much the language of the true flirt. At the end of the day, it's a game, and it's meant to be fun. Think lusty body contact with a playful push and pull of limber limbs, shameless grins, wandering thighs and lingering eyes. It's powerful but understated, sexual but sensual, saucy but sultry. *Got that?*

*Fun Fact No 1: Women who are approached confidently and treated with courtesy and respect are more likely to have a drink with you, go out with you – and bring you breakfast in bed.*

*Fun Fact No 2: I've got the best boyfriend in Britain. The other one's in Australia. Kidding!* ☺

## Internationally Recognized Flirting Gestures

Now that you've acknowledged that English women give off smoke-signals, rather than, you know, proper Green Light signals, you need to figure a way to work around it.

***30-Second Guide:*** There's a cute girl at the bar and she's looking right at you. You think to yourself, *"What the devil? Girls never look at me! I must have a big green jellyfish on my face!*

But there's no denying that she's glancing over your way. And then, just as quickly, she looks away.

But…wait! She looks over again.

*Right now part of you is screaming: "But that never happens!",* while failing to take into account that it never happens because you never pay attention! Once you take off your blinkers, it will start happening all the time. It's up to you to be prepared so that when it happens, you act on it!

You catch her mid-flight. But bewilderingly, stubbornly, nervously you refuse to meet her gaze – instead, you look the other way!

In her mind it's all gone pear-shaped.

*"He saw me!"* she stage-whispers to her friend.

But the truth is, you have no idea what's going on (well you are a guy and all). You look behind you, next to you and over your shoulder. You wonder who she was looking at. And then the penny drops!

She was looking at YOU.

You didn't look back at her because you didn't twig. Meanwhile all hell broke loose.

*"He KNOWS I fancy him"* She hisses to her friend as she flounces out throwing you a dirty look. *"Screw him!"*

As far as she's concerned, you had your chance, and you blew it buddy!

And you missed the whole thing which is a real shame because it's Game Over.

That's if she's a Shy Flirt. But even if she is an accomplished flirt, and she really makes a play for you, half the time you still don't get it!

*So, why is it so hard to get across that we like you?*

It's like I said earlier, most of you wouldn't know a flirting gesture if it leapt up and thumped you on the nose! And who knows why! Maybe you're shy or paralysed by fear; or you're overly concerned with how you're coming across and therefore ridiculously self-conscious. As such you're at a loss for what to say or what to do.

Added to that, you're probably not paying enough attention, or the right sort of attention. You're too busy focusing on what you'll say next, so you can be cleverer and more hilarious than us.

*Sound familiar?*

If so, you need to adjust your attitude, because as of now, it's all about her!

You need to step up to the plate. You need to watch, listen and pay attention. If you so much as get a whiff that someone is giving you a sign, however subtle, then it's your job to volley it back.

It's called 'Transmitting.' She sends. You receive. Get it?

**Flirt Watchdog:** You're out, you're flirting and you're fabulous. Once you spot this luminous lady, it's *Lights, Camera, Action!*

✓ *You brush her arm with every hilarious punch-line*

✓ *Make unwavering eye-contact*

✓ *Respond with emphatic nods and smiles*

✓ *Move in closer with every sentence and smile*

But, wait a minute: Are you paying attention to the signals she's sending back? Because even if she's not an explosion of big hair, shiny lips and swinging hips, BUT she's playing with her hair and batting her eyes and being a bit fidgety, then she's doing her best dammit, to get the message across – and you've got to act on that! Because if you make the No 1 rookie mistake of missing the signals, then you're only having half the fun – and, you're only doing half the job!

Or maybe you're just like three quarters of the British male population, who according to UK research, have no idea when women are flirting with them.

### Fact Check

✓ In a study carried out by psychologist Professor Richard Wiseman in 2009, British blokes were scientifically revealed to be the *least romantic* on the planet. *Gasp!*

✓ According to the National Statistics 2010 Census report, their were18.5 million single adults – nearly 1/3 of the population!

✓ As well as being the divorce capital of the world, Britain also has the greatest number of adulterers (just thought you might like to know that).

✓ We also have the fastest rising number of STD's!

# Body Language Maths

Body language is what Pussycat Doll, Nicole Scherzinger has in spades when she slithers onto our TV screens all limbs, legs and lusciousness. It's an intricate network of non-verbal messages that we send via our physical mannerisms – either consciously or subconsciously. It's talking without words. Or in this case, flirting without words.

Experts say that between seventy to ninety percent of all human communication comes from body language. When we meet someone for the first time, we form an opinion based on how they present ourselves, they way they stand and sit and hurl themselves about. It's the same when we go on dates, which is why they can be so nerve-wracking. Just the thought of being assessed by someone you barely know is enough to get you breaking out into a sweat isn't it? That's why it pays to know the basics.

Did you know for instance that crossing your arms can make you look defensive and aggressive? *"Yes"* you sigh. *"We learnt that before we were toilet trained."* OK fine, smarty-pants. Well what about the girl with a curl who twirls and swirls and smiles coquettishly. What's she saying? The correct answer is of course *You. Me. How 'bout it!'*

Having control of your body language might not lead directly to the love of your life necessarily, but if all you have to do to improve your chances is be more aware of it, it can't hurt can it? Especially when a hot babe appears on your radar. It's moments like these that you need to focus on the vibe – what's going down? Is she giving you sly little hints by:

- ✓ Flicking her hair
- ✓ Fidgeting with her necklace
- ✓ Doing the touchy-feelies – a playful pat here, a fun punch there
- ✓ Drawing attention to her most bootylicious body parts
- ✓ Giving you lots of cheeky little glances

This might be the Diet Coke talking, but if she is doing any or all of the above, there's a good chance she's trying to tell you something. If that's the case, she's waiting for YOU to make a move. The minute you get the ball, you need to lob it back in a heartbeat. From there, it's simply a game of 'mirroring'. Or, as I like to think of it…monkey see…monkey do.

Mirroring is a technique used in most social situations, equally suitable for job interviews or first dates. It's what you do to put someone at ease. So if you're sat with someone and they are very poised and still, then in theory, your body language would pick up on that and reflect it. Likewise if someone is super animated and gesticulating madly, then you would adopt a similar energy – or not.

Bear with me here... because while mirroring works on a subconscious level, there are many instances where if you over think it, or take it too literally, you will overdo it and end up looking plain silly. For instance if you're a calm, cool, collected type, you're not going to throw yourself around in a frenzied whirl of body language just because you're chatting with someone who's like that – that would just look weird right? It has to be subtle with the end result being that by picking up on someone's basic mannerisms, you're showing you're on their wavelength which is great – so long as you're mindful that it's all about balance.

You may have heard the expression, '*Invading his/her body space*'. This refers to an invisible force field we have around ourselves to protect from unwanted physical intimacy. Typically if an acquaintance or a stranger moves within that barrier, we flinch and retreat by shuffling backwards. Rule of thumb, if you lean in even just a fraction closer than what is culturally acceptable; you're likely to make someone feel uncomfortable. Of course that all changes within a romantic setting where a case of leaning in nice and close is enough to give the game away.

The knack of reading body language starts with self-awareness. You'd be amazed by how much you can convey, or reveal by what your body says, but you need to know what you're doing. Here in Britain it's not like in other parts of the world, say some European cities for instance, where men are exceptionally comfortable when it comes to the touchy-feely stuff. Especially in Italy, where it's not always, ahem, appreciated. I think a certain Mr Berlusconi might know a thing or two about that! Likewise in Spain where the men are also incredibly tactile and happy to express their affection with a variety of playful gestures – getting my nose tugged was one I experienced with alarming regularity (I bet if someone in London tried that, we'd flatten them!). Another Spanish gesture is to put your hands to the side of your head to indicate that it's time to go to bed and sleep – or otherwise. Hmmm...very playful and, or suggestive.

### *Technical Term of the Day: Metronomic*

Your personal body language has the power to make someone gravitate towards, or away, from you. Look out for the gestures that people use to make a really strong point. Or where they're trying to tell you something. Get the hang of it by familiarising yourself with traditional defiant and passionate and angry gestures. Study couples the next time you're out people watching and see who's holding the power card. Better still watch the televised replay of Rupert Murdoch as he was interrogated by British Parliament – he didn't say a lot, but boy his metronomic gesturing said plenty!

- ✓ Slap your hand down
- ✓ Drum your fingers across the table
- ✓ Beat your brow
- ✓ Point your finger
- ✓ Clap your hands together triumphantly
- ✓ Punch your fist into the air

### *Are You Flirting Back?*

It may well be that you're good at initiating contact and setting up a date, but what happens then? Do you literally crumble and fall when it comes to the actual tic-tacs of what to do? Especially if she's coming across as miracle of miracles – a wee bit flirty. And how do you know if she's flirting just for you, or if she does it with everyone she meets? What are you meant to do? Do you flirt back? If so, how much is too much? If she does the touchy-feelies, should you do the same, or is that just lame?

These are the common quandaries which millions of you have gone nearly mental trying to figure out. Of course there are no black and white answers, suffice it to say, the best thing is to familiarise yourself with the signals. That means learning through trial and error. That way you'll get a feel for what's really going down.

And who ever knows the exact moment of when to push forward and pull back; or when you're being too cool, or coming across as too keen. The best defence is to trust your gut instinct and rely on common sense. It's like I said at the beginning, you will screw up at some point, that's a given, but you can't let that stop you from trying. You know what they say, no guts, no glory. And really, so what if you screw up. What's the worst thing that can happen? On the bright side, you'll be better positioned for next time. The trick is to have a handle on the main components so you know what you're looking out for. A key component of which is – eye-contact.

# Eye-Contact

If you want to seduce anyone, the first thing you need is seriously good eye-contact, otherwise you can forget all about making a good impression. And since we do not typically make excessive direct eye-contact in our day-to-day, it can make you feel self-conscious, especially if you fancy someone. Sod's Law! If you've ever travelled on the tube in London, then you know what I'm talking about – what a shocker! But that's different to a social situation when you're out and about hoping to meet someone, because in that situation, if you can't look someone dead in the eye, they're likely to jump to all the wrong conclusions and think that you're all shifty like.

But, and here's the thing, if you can look at her, really look at her – and resist the urge to look over her shoulder, at your feet, or longingly at her bazookas, you've got a good shot of making her feel special, and that's half the battle won. Likewise if you stumble across a lone lady sitting in a cafe sipping a Crappucino and reading '*Lonely Planet Guide to Greece*', and you make some good eye-contact along with a killer opening line: *"I've always found the Time Out City Guides more reliable"* then you will have kick-started things very nicely indeed.

## *Her Point of View*

And don't think it's just the men who struggle. I coach loads of women who find it just as tough when it comes to eye-contact – especially with those they fancy. It's awful too, because if someone's shy and awkward and finds it impossible to make good eye-contact, precisely because they fancy you, then clearly you can't depend on eye-contact as an accurate gauge. You can only use it as a guideline. So, if some fanceable woman is studiously avoiding your gaze, rather than assuming you've got no chance, you could give her the benefit of the doubt and look for other signs of what's really going on. This should help you figure out whether she's acting that way because she feels shy, or she really doesn't fancy you.

### *A Step-by-Step Guide To Making Your Intentions Known*

✓ Glance over her way – up to three times or more

✓ Hold her eye-contact when you first meet, especially potent if you do it whilst shaking her hand. *'Phwoar!'* She'll be thinking.

✓ Now look at her; really LOOK at her. Take in the colour of her eyes, the size of the pupil, the length of the lashes, the shape of the brow...all of it.

✓ Pay attention to her eye-contact. Is she holding your gaze? Or giving you one of those soft, gooey looks? Or is she looking over your shoulder – everywhere except at you?

✓ If you like what you see, and you want to let her know, let your gaze drop to her lips – she'll soon know what's on your mind!


## *When Someone Avoids Your Gaze*

Gaze Aversion is what happens when someone refuses to meet your eyes. It could be for one of two reasons: either they really don't like you, or they don't trust you. Or, it's the complete opposite and they want to bonk your brains out! For that reason they can't risk looking at you – for fear of a heart attack!

If that happens, you need to look for other signals to back up one theory or the other. Use your instinct here. If you're sensing anger or defensiveness, then that's not a very convincing case of someone being head-over-heels in lust with you is it? If on the other hand you sense something warm and heartfelt, then you're on the right street. Take the time to figure out what's going on to avoid one or both of you missing out on something potentially amazing.

### How Much Eye-Contact Is She Giving You?

### *Blow You Out of Your Sox Flirting Tip #1*

She gives you the Peek-a-Boo Gaze, either face-to-face or from a distance. She instinctively knows the power behind the tantalizing effect of being "peeped-at".

*Top Tip*: She keeps her lips pursed and her head tilted ever so slightly when she smiles. She lowers her eyes and then looks upward, hitting you with the full force of her oh-so seductive gaze. Think a coquettish Princess Di. Move in quickly when she does this!

### *Blow You Out of Your Sox Flirting Tip #2*

*Eyebrow bobbing*: She raises one or two brows with a slash of oo-er naughtiness thrown in, followed by a rapid lowering to the normal position. This is most effective combined with a smile and strong eye contact. It indicates a cheeky and often suggestive message in the vein of national treasure Barbara Windsor *Carry On* film. To best demonstrate is Ms Angelina Jolie – high priestess of the brow flash.

*Top Tip: Used in conjunction with the Peek-a-Book Gaze described above.*

**Paying Attention:** You use every bit of willpower you have to ignore the over inflated Pammy Anderson look-alike over in the corner. It's tricky though, in fact this mission is impossible! But keep the focus. You're keeping your eye on the big prize!

### *What Else Should You Look Out For?*

✓ *Glancing:* She flashes a series of short darting glances which usually occur in sets of 3 for around 3-5 seconds long. The secret is to let you catch her looking and then to do it again. *'Cheeky wench!'* you think!

✓ *Secret gazing:* She looks at you and lets her eyes focus – like seeing you for the first time.

### *Where to look when she flaunts a cleavage like the Grand Canyon*

If a woman in your radar is spilling out of her little black dress with a top cut so low that displays all of her show stopping chesticles like the most delectable dish on the buffet table, then, by all means have a sneaky peek, but do you mind not making it a full on ogle? It doesn't matter how low the top, or how sumptuous the bosom, it just not gentlemanly to stare. And stare. And stare. Particularly if you like this woman and you're hoping for more than a dirty one-nighter. Of course, if that's all you're after, and you have no regards for the woman's feelings or future happiness, then you're reading the wrong book.

*Top Tip:* Experts say that people look to the left if they are telling the truth. If the eyes look up and to the right, it is said that these are thoughts that are constructed – in other words a lie. *Hmmmmm....interesting!*

Riddle: *What is Flirting?*

A) **Body Language?**

B) **Eye Contact?**

C) **Something one only does when one is absolutely stonkered?**

*Answer: A. B & C!*

---

*Flirting is what we do when we're feeling playful and mischievous and we want to let someone know we think they're fun.*

*Flirting is NOT when we say:*

*"Come back to mine. There'll be no fooling around. Just full sex."* — *Hugh Grant, Bridget Jones*

## What Signals Should You Be On The Look-Out For?

Sexual attraction is about transmitting signals with strong body language and direct eye-contact. What is she saying and is *her message clear and direct?* Or has it become muddled through the puddle of sexual politics? Whether it's the way she lowers her voice, the curve of her smile, the tilt of her adorable head – she's transmitting a direct message. The key is to maintain an eagle eye, but also to be patient. It may take a little while before you're good enough to decipher the code, especially when you're busy beaming out your own lusty message, but soon it will feel like the most natural thing in the word. It would be a crime to let all that sexually charged power go to waste!

Once upon a time three of the hottest actors in the world got together and have been known as *Charlie's Angels* ever since: Drew Barrymore, Cameron Diaz and Lucy Liu are famous for their killer bodies and their miles and miles of cheeky smiles. But how do you know if a smile is genuine? You need to watch closely next time you saunter over to say, *"Alright Gels?"*

### *A Good Flirt Knows How to Frame Her Best Assets*

### *The Cheeky Smile*

✓ Does her smile reach all the way to her eyes?

    ✗ If it only stretches to the corners of her mouth, then she is not having a great time – however much she is playing the part.

✓ Is she is smiling in a mysterious and secretive way?

✓ A way that makes it clear that she is aware of, and very much in favour of, the sexual tension going on here?

✓ Well c'mon – that's a sign!

*Mind your manners: A smile is not an invitation to harass!*

*Handnique: Think belly-dancing. Think sex. Think Shakira!*

A good flirt knows only too well that graceful hand movements can be mesmerizing, not to mention highly *erotic*. We all know a good set of hands can do marvellous things...*Hmmm?* Does she drum her fingers lightly on the table bringing attention to sculpted hands and delicate wrists? Does she flaunt them lavishly when she's in full storytelling mode, letting her beautifully manicured nails dance as melodiously as if she were playing the piano? Look for the giveaways that she's interested in showing you more...

### Head & Shoulders

➤ She plays with a necklace that settles tantalisingly in her décolleté

➤ She poses at her best angle, tilts her head and showcases her profile

➤ She cups her chin in her hands and frames her face in a classic Audrey Hepburn pose

### Leg-nique
*Think Naomi Campbell (when she's not throwing telephones)*

➤ She rests her hands under her upper legs when she sits down

➤ She slides her foot in and out of a backless shoe

➤ She entwines her shapely legs, displaying her taut calves

### Giveaways That Tell You She's TROUBLE

➤ *She's wearing a t-shirt that says: 'GOLD DIGGA!'*

➤ *She comes on way too strong*

➤ *She's flirting with you, but shagging your best mate*

## 30 Second Guide to...Object Focused Actions

This is as cheesy as you like so go ahead and laugh readers but, you know all that stuff you hear about girls stroking the phallic stem of their wine glass and sucking on their Bacardi Breezer bottle like there's no tomorrow to give you a glimpse of what's on their mind, well it's true! Didn't you see Madonna famously fellate the water bottle in that scene from *In Bed With Madonna?*

If you've been paying attention in the movies you would have noticed how the femme fatales touch themselves in those erogenous spots they might like to be touched. A hand on the hips, the lips, the t*** – you get the picture. Not that they do it intentionally mind, it happens on a subconscious level. Watch closely and see if you can spot the way women manipulate phallic symbols. If you find a whole host torpedoing your way anytime soon, then you know she is flirting with you. *Oh yes she is!!*

### What does it mean if you have 'closed body language'?

'Closed' body language generally means you're not using your body to express yourself clearly. 'Open' body language means you're using all available limbs and body parts to express yourself and show that you're having fun – that's flirting!

Guys often ask how they are supposed to pull theses moves out of the bag if it's not their thing. And I get that. Especially if you've grown up in a household where emotions were not freely displayed and there was no affection thrown around. Of course it can be tricky to snap your fingers and transform into that person. But, there are ways to improve and if you feel like something out of the Thunderbirds – you need to do something radical to loosen up. In Step 4 we talk about ways to 'unblock.'

### Standing Still

They say that those with the *most* power move around the least, and say the least – that's because they've got confidence in truckloads and don't feel they need to prove anything. Having said that, those who are keen on someone but as still and as lifeless as a plank, will inevitably come across as a plank. Besides how can you tell if someone's got the hots for you if they're not larking about, or making a massive effort to be funny and cute? If you opt to stand dead still, barely responding to anything she says or does, she's likely to get the hump because it seems like you could give a rat's about her. But if that's not the case and you genuinely want to keep her around, you need to be more animated.

*Rule of thumb: Don't over gesticulate. Don't under gesticulate.*

There are no foolproof rules at work here and nothing is set in stone. A lot of what we say and do is instinctual; it's just a matter of becoming attuned to that process. If it gets to the point where you're not hanging on to her every word, or even pretending to be enthralled by her goddess like presence, she will get the feeling that you're just not that into her. That's because she's sensitive and she doubts herself. She also comes with every insecurity in the book.

Try leaning your body around to face hers and form a little a semi-circle which acts as a barrier to the rest of the world; a space where it's just you and her. Put the spotlight on her and make her feel like the Queen of freakin' Sheba. Do it because you can. Do it because she'll feel amazing. Do it, because, it might just change your life!

## *Scoreboard*

If you get any of the following signals on high rotation you're in with a good chance. Is she:

✓   *Smiling: a wide, open mouthed toothy smile*

✓   *Sitting up straight where everything appears firmer and tauter*

✓   *Rocking back and forth towards you – targeting you fair and square*

✓   *Gazing into your eyes with a lazy, half smile*

✓   *Twirling her hair around while holding your eye-contact*

✓   *Initiating a fun game of "touchy-feelies"*

✓   *Watching every little thing you do*

✓   *Flipping, flicking and tossing her hair*

✓   *Playing with accessories: jewellery, trinkets and necklace*

✓   *Posing, preening and pouting*

✓   *Licking her lips*

✓   *Drawing attention to off limits body parts*

✓   *Positioning her hands around the pelvic/hip area*

✓   *Leaning in towards you*

✓   *Tilting her neck and head*

✓   *Directing eye contact to take in both your eyes and lips*

✓ *Raising both brows (in the manner of the Carry On films)*

✓ *Dishing out all the subtle – and not so subtle – gestures*

✓ *Touching your arm, your hand, your leg!*

✓ *Wearing her 'I'm up for it' T-shirt*

### Listen up! Does She:

✓ *Lower her voice to create a low, sexy vibe only you can hear?*

✓ *Lean in and whispers, brushing your arm before pulling away?*

✓ *Let out a long, deep sigh?*

✓ *Make a purring sound?*

✓ *Raise or lower the volume of her voice to match yours?*

## Spot The Flirt

Whilst I'm out on the job in London's cafes and bars, I have the opportunity to observe – OK – eavesdrop on every kind of scenario imaginable. Over coffee at Costa one morning, I found myself deeply absorbed in the following.

It was clear from the outset that this 20-something couple were just friends but they had loads of chemistry and boy, was I in for a treat. The girl entertained her friend by telling him how she was – wait for it – naked in the hostel dorm room when this guy, a mutual friend of theirs, burst in. She'd just got out of the shower. She took off the towel. She was applying body moisturiser…the door opened... and on and on and on. It sounded like an erotic scene from an X-Rated film! The guy, bless his cotton socks, was quiet, just listening and grinning and taking it all in as you do, looking a little flushed here and there. Afterwards she toddled off to the ladies. He got out his iPhone and called his mate. *"I don't know what to do"* he said, *"She is so f****** hot, but she only likes me as a friend."*

And there I was listening away, all the while thinking, *'Get with the program dude!'* If any woman gives you that amount of detail about her nekkid or semi-nekkid state, then I'm sorry, but she is putting that picture in your mind for a reason. Read between the lines already!! My good golly gosh, a more masterful example of flirting I have never seen.

Another morning, I watched as a totally gorgeous English girl had coffee with a really cute English guy who was clearly besotted by her. As they chatted, she leaned over and lifted his wrist to look more closely at a tattoo on his inner forearm. Then she launched into a sweet little story about the time she *had her nipple pierced!* I watched for his reaction. Smooth as could be, he told her he had a pierced nipple also. He asked if she had any tattoos. She said she did, but she'd show him later.

*Round of applause please!*

50

***Listen out for clues to see if she's flirting. Does she mention:***

✓  Her boob slippage

✓  Her concern with a too small skirt

✓  That some other guy is hot for her

✓  Something, anything, to do with being in bed, alone, naked

✓  Ditto the shower

*She's playing with you dude!*


## What's the difference between a flirt and a monster prick tease?

Hmmm, I was wondering when you'd ask. As we've already established, it can be hard finding a girl who's prepared to drop her defences and wear her heart on her sleeve. But there's the other end of the spectrum as well. So, let's talk about different kinds of flirts because, fun fact, there are loads!

First up there's the slutty flirt – no doubt you would have come across her late one night in some seedy club. Then there's the social-flirt, she just wants to be loved by everyone. There's the do-anything to get-ahead-flirt, the man-eating flirt, the revenge flirt, the power flirt, the manipulative flirt and of course, drum roll please...the PRICK TEASE. And while this may not be the girl you choose to take home to meet your mum, it pays to be aware because...

You know her. She's the one who uses everything she's got. She's not necessarily the best looking, but she knows how to work it. She flirts outrageously and gets off on making you believe that you've got a chance. The problem is she doesn't necessarily fancy you; she just wants top up her ego. She wants to win! She'll lead you right up the garden-path and then drop you cold. How can you avoid her? You can't. She's out there. And she will find you.

## What Signals Is SHE On The Look Out For?

Since a big part of what we communicate is via our body language, you need to know what *she's looking for.* Assuming she's flirting, in her own subtle (read invisible) way, then you need to be dishing out the moves that *she recognises as flirting.* I know this may not necessarily sit well with you, but work with me here! She doesn't expect you to be the *complete* Casanova, but, she does expect a response.

Initially you would respond by demonstrating the classic *"I'm into you"* full frontal moves. Just don't get carried away. Start by twisting your torso around so you are facing her. Point your feet towards her – and look at her, really look at her. This is the way that hi-camp touchy-feely men communicate with women. You just have to look at Russell Brand (who clearly isn't gay, but is very in touch with his feminine side). He uses it as his Secret Weapon to ingratiate himself to women.

For the record, I feel it is the ladies place to take the lead in the touchy-feelies. In other words, if there's any touching to be done, she should be the one to initiate it. Having said that, I know of many men who swear by giving her a pat on the arm or the shoulder on the basis that it breaks down defences and reinforces feelings of trust and familiarity. If it comes naturally and you think you're smooth enough to pull it off – and charm us half to death in the process – then go for it. It's not pretty. It's not subtle, but it's definitely flirting! Other ways to let her know you're keen are quite simply...

✓   *The twinkle in your eye*

✓   *The way you angle yourself towards her*

✓   *Your hands on your hips*

✓   *A raised eye-brow*

✓   *A cheeky grin followed by a wink*

***She'll know she's in with a chance if you do any of the following:***
- Belly goes in and the shoulders go back as you *stride* across the room.
- You angle your body so you're facing her full frontal
- You're up for a dance
- Your mate simply vanishes
- You say you're going to the toilet – and you come back
- You initiate a full body bear-hug when she says goodbye

***Likewise if you use any of these Key Indicators:***
- ✓ Make the initial approach
- ✓ Invade her personal space
- ✓ Hold extended eye-contact
- ✓ Stroke her hair
- ✓ Play with her accessories
- ✓ Mimic her body movements
- ✓ Isolate yourself from your friends
- ✓ Walk by and look back over your shoulder
- ✓ Do show and tell with your tattoo
- ✓ Lean over and touch her tattoo
- ✓ Play the touchy-feelies with her hand, her wrist – her whatever!
- ✓ Use the furry warmth of your hand to wipe the raindrop from her face

***Or use any of the following giveaways….***

- ✓ *Lip licking:* We tend to unconsciously draw attention to our mouth if we're physically attracted to someone – especially if we're thinking about what we might like to do a little later. It might be a single lip-lick, wetting the lip, or running the tongue around the entire lip.

- ✓ *Hair flipping*: Or the male equivalent. Push your fingers through your hair, stroke your beard, or play with your 'tache. Your fidgeting suggests you've got the heebie-jeebies bad.
- ✓ *Half smiling:* Shoot her a knowing half-smile with clear and direct eye contact. A strong hint that you're in lust with her.
- ✓ *Whispering:* Lean over and speak softly into her ear and create a secret, intimate world just for the two of you. *Mmmmm.*
- ✓ *Primping, preening or peacocking*: Smooth down your clothing even if it doesn't need any adjusting. You want to look your best for her.
- ✓ *Shirt sleeve hiking:* The top of your shirt sleeve rides up to expose a little more of that strong, muscular forearm. *What a show off!*
- ✓ *Show her the goods:* Put your hands on your hips, or in your belt loops to accentuate your, erm, nether regions. You *cannot* keep still!
- ✓ *Object caressing:* Manhandle your keys, play with your lighter or anything you can wrap your mitts around - *in lieu of her.*
- ✓ *Leg opener:* Open those legs even wider. *Phwoar.*
- ✓ *Posturing:* The way you're sitting and standing becomes more er, erect. *Say no more.*
- ✓ *A pat on the hand*: known as a Nappy Pat, may come across as condescending and completely non-sexual

### *And, only if you can get away with it, the OTT stuff:*

- ➢ Dip an imaginary cap
- ➢ Salute her
- ➢ Bow to her
- ➢ Blow her a kiss
- ➢ Kiss her hand
- ➢ Raise your glass and toast your future happiness. Together!

## Watchdog Alert

➤ Closed and guarded body language denotes tension and a cagey personality

➤ Tongue protruding from inside of the cheek could mean you're hiding the truth

➤ Power walking: big steps and swinging arms will make you appear bigger than you are

➤ Tightly pursed lips equals anxiety

➤ Physically moving away equals, fear, discomfort, the desire for distance

➤ Stabbing gestures denote seriousness; you mean business, and feel a tad aggressive

➤ Feet turned away suggests the desire to get away!


**And Remember:** *Doing the touchy-feelies doesn't mean pawing. A clumsy pat on the hand or a bruising arm around the shoulder will set the wrong tone altogether. We want playful not pawing!*

# Rrrrejection

Why is it that men think they have the monopoly on rejection? There is nothing predominately male about the fear of rejection, just as there is nothing predominately female about it – it's just as dire for all of us.

So why would *anyone* want to put themselves through the indignity and humiliation and stress that goes with the process of trying to find The One? Well there are a lot of reasons, namely that in order to pursue red hot romance, one must prepare for rejection of the very worst kind. I'm not trying to put the fear of god into you, but in spoilsport Dating Doctor mode, I should share this sobering piece warning of the dangers, so that you may enjoy your flirting foray all the more.

I understand the pain of rejection, who doesn't? We've all been there. But you need to be realistic and see it for what it is – a numbers game. Rejection is a very real part of our lives, no matter whether your name is George Clooney, or Jack the Lad. We've all been through it and we've all lived to tell the tale. So will you – provided you don't let the demons screw you up.

Think back to your earliest playground memories: was there ever a moment when your fantasy playmate wouldn't even look at you, let alone play with you? When she cried when you came within ten feet of her and squawked: *"Take it away because it's smelly and it stinks and it's horrible."* Sound familiar? Yes I thought so. That's where it all began.

**Hello *Mills & Boon*!** There will always be obstacles and challenges to overcome before the leading man gets his lady. Emotional conflict meets inner turmoil. You know the drill:

- Boy meets Girl
- Boy chases girl
- Girl causes boy nothing but grief
- Boy backs off
- Girl cleans up her act
- Boy takes girl back

And there's your happy ending! It is genuinely baffling, but somehow, the less sense it makes, the better it works out in the end. It doesn't get easier as we get older. If anything it gets harder. Sorry, I'm just telling it how it is. Nor does it go to plan most of the time, that's life, otherwise known as Sod's Law. And since we don't come equipped with the faculties to deal with rejection, it can be tough. Especially for guys who are hotwired to be aggressive and competitive when it comes to all things bats and balls, career and cricket – but so very easily deflated when it comes to women. Chances are you will be as badly affected by a brisk rejection that comes from a clumsy approach in a noisy club, than if you were officially listed for the *Really Bad Sex Award*.

There is a bizarre tendency when it comes to all things mating and dating, to try to control every aspect of it. But that's never going to happen. Think about it. We accept rejection every day, in some form or another. We accept that not every job interview we apply for will be successful and not all material things are within our reach, yet we expect everyone we fancy to laugh hysterically at our lame gags and fall in lust with us. Then when they don't, we are crushed beyond redemption. Blimey! It's this kind of pressure that makes our encounters so fraught. We worry ourselves sick that someone won't fancy us, and that makes us crazy. But really there's no logic here. You don't have to appeal to everyone from Wales to Wolverhampton, it's just not necessary – or realistic.

## Lost in Manslation

Sometimes it's not even the rejection that's so fearsome; it's the mere thought of it that's enough to put anyone off. But what is the basis of your fear? And what's the worst thing that can happen if someone kicks you to the kerb? Is it the shame of losing face? Being turned down? Being fobbed off? I suspect it's a little of all of the above. We're only human. We all have feelings. We might like to think we're automated robots when it comes to this stuff, but we're not. It does hurt when someone sniggers in your face when you've just tried to be pleasant. I get that. The only response is to take it in your stride and take it like a man. You have no cause for real fear – once you take out all the bullshit that is. Save that energy, and focus on making a meaningful bond with someone real; someone who appreciates you. Because really, who cares if you say the wrong thing, or snort rather too loudly when you laugh? No-one's testing you. No-one's grading you. This is not a life or death situation. You can bet your bottom pound she's not perfect. She's just some girl. She's not judging you. She's too worried if her Bum Looks Big In This.

And honestly, you can take all the Anti-Rejection Pills you want, but you're better off to anticipate the worst case scenario, because nom de dieu! It will happen. And when it does, there's only one thing to do. Stop, breathe and take stock of the situation. We've all been there. We've all experienced this heart attack inducing shite. The trick is to stay calm. Switch your internal panic alarm off. Pick yourself up, dust yourself down, take a big breath, wave your SOS flag and get back out there! If you see that vicious wench again, ignore her. Don't let her know she's upset you. It's not a L'Oreal advertisement, and *she's not worth it!*

Once you've got the right attitude, and you're calm and focused, you will see how this can be a relatively painless process. Bottom line, you need an attitude that doesn't flip at the sight of a hot babe – which can be hard. You see her and she's so hot you want to party her into the ground right there and then. But instead, stay cool.

The key is not to take it too seriously. It's all just fun and games. But it takes a real man, a strong man, a hard man to get that maracas shaking message over the line and into someone's mind, but if anyone can do it, you can. *Keep telling yourself. Believe in yourself!* You don't have to come across all hot and heavy. Just give her a sign. If she gets it she gets it, if she doesn't, she doesn't. Once you get the hang of it, you'll be addicted. Just watch and see.

***Fun Fact: Rejection Means Nothing To Successful Guys.***

# What Women Want

I already knew that 33-year-old Alison was a big hitter. Tiny but titanic, she was loud and funny – when she was with the girls – but once she was out of her comfort zone, she went to ground. Her impish hair and petite frame could surely not be threatening to any man, woman or child, yet during the three years she'd been single, she has never been approached. Gradually, it's taken its toll on her personality. These days she is completely overwhelmed by the dating arena which she says feels like 'entering a shark pool'. As for the notion of meeting men, her question is, *'But, how?!'* From Alison's point of view, it's not getting any easier. If anything, it's getting harder. This is what she says when I ask her what the problem is:

*"When I go out in London, it's to meet up with friends. If I'm busy chatting to them and catching up, I'm not going to be checking out every bloke that walks by! Hugh Grant could be sitting ten feet away and I wouldn't have a clue. I think it's easy to ignore what's going on around you because, let's face it no-one's very friendly. So it's not like when I go to the pub I'm going to meet someone. It would never occur to me. And it has never happened! So I don't look for it. And it doesn't look for me!"*

I dig a little deeper and ask what happens if she gets noticed by guys.

*"Well it doesn't happen… Because if someone looks at me, I look away and then they give up! Once or twice I have caught someone's eye, but then, it feels weird, so I just look away really quickly… I wish I could smile at them, or return the look, but it seems like every time I do, they go and talk to someone else. Someone prettier. And that makes me feel bad. So why should I bother?"*

Because she's not used to it, the whole eye-contact thing feels confronting. The worst thing is that if Alison does catch someone's eye, she'll convince herself that they're looking at her by mistake. That's her self-esteem talking. She refuses to believe that a cute guy could be checking her out. So, rather than wait for him to look away, and then ignore her, she looks away first. That way she can't get rejected. Which is a crime because once you get chatting to her she's smiley and lively and fun. It's getting to know her that's the hard part.

That's the problem. All well and good, but what's the solution? If Alison was better at handling eye-contact and if she had more confidence, she would be more likely to make a connection. And then, YOU, being the legend that you are, might be more inclined to smile and say hi. But since she's not giving out the signals, you're not making a move. Bottom line, if you want to get to know the Alison's of the world, the only way it's going to happen is if you take the *WTF!* approach and go in without fear. Of course it's only the real super troopers amongst you will be willing and able to do that. I didn't say it was fair, I'm just telling it the way it is.

Alicia is in her mid 30s and a dead ringer for *Desperate Housewife*, Eva Longoria. In spite of her gorgeousness, Alicia is one of the shyest people I've met. During our night out, she stayed stubbornly in her shell. Whatever spin you put on it, taking a risk is not her thing. But to look at her with that amazing head of bed-hair and the dress with a killer neckline that says *Grrrrr,* you'd just assume that she was massively confident, or taken, one or the other. But she's not. Not on either count. She is very single and very available. Further proof that you must never presume anything! The problem is that she feels terribly self-conscious about it. She doesn't understand why she is single. She knows she's attractive because she gets the looks, but since she hates flaunting her availability, there's a 'Stay Away' vibe that pulsates around her, so of course, no-one comes within spitting distance. As a result she's left alone. That makes her feel more unattractive, even though deep down she knows she's avoiding the attention. She may be rocking a dangerously low neckline but it's not much use if you can't catch her eye. It's a Catch 22. And the only guy who's going to break through her force field is the guy who's got the courage to hang around long enough to start a conversation. Once she starts chatting she's OK, it's getting her started that takes some work.

Fran is a 28-year-old researcher who's the spitting image of a young Janet Jackson. In a word, she's gorgeous. She's also as shy as a kitten. Yet, with her thick black hair tumbling around her shoulders, her dusky, dewy skin; bright, glossy eyes and clad head-to -toe in skin-tight black – you wouldn't think so. That's because she's a knock out. To look at her, you'd think she was getting hit on every minute of the day. Yet, since she arrived from New Zealand two years ago, she's not had one single guy approach her. Not one! *'WHAT THE FREAK IS GOING ON GUYS?'* I ask what she thinks the problem is. She furrows her brow and says this:

*"I don't know. I think I scare them away. Maybe I look too serious. The funny thing is that I'm not, I'm just shy. But I can't help the way I look. If I'm in a conversation with someone, I tend to have my serious face on. I can't help it. I can see why it could turn guys off though."*

So it's Fran's serious face that's scaring the boys away. *Aha!* Now we're getting somewhere. Can you see how silly this is? I mean really? Fran wears her heart on her sleeve because that's one of the quirks that makes her Fran and as a result she doesn't get approached. Ever! *Gah Fury!*

But of course there's more to it than that. After spending time with this gorgeous creature, I learnt that ever since high school, Fran has thought of herself as quiet and shy – that's just who she is. She prefers to warm up slowly to new people or situations. As with many shy people, she's just really bad at small talk; it takes time to cut through. It's easy to see how you could mistakenly think that she is standoffish or aloof. But once you get to know her it's clear that Fran is a genuine and caring person, a brilliant listener with a surprisingly lewd wit.

I also noticed that she does have a sort of unfortunate tendency to settle into 'frowny' mode when she's in conversation. When she's paying attention and listening really hard, her eyes crinkle and her brow furrows – that's her default position. Nothing wrong with that except that it stops you guys in your tracks! Even if you really want to approach, you see her with that frowny face when she's chatting with whoever and you feel the fear and stay the hell away which only makes things worse. Because the more Fran is ignored, the more her confidence dips. The more her confidence dips, the less likely she is to smile. The less likely she is to smile, the less likelihood of you going over to say hi. Do you see the bullocks here?

I know. I know. What are you meant to do? Make an ass of yourself on the basis that some ridiculously hot girl is shy and not stuck up at all? Look I'm not saying that's the solution and I'm not pretending to have all the answers. I just want to show that things aren't always what they seem on the surface. There are times, many, many times when you might be pleasantly surprised; just as there are many times when you will not. Doomed if you do and doomed if you don't. Bloody hell 'eh!

The thing is that these are not isolated cases. Fran's story is broadly representative of many, many situations I deal with. I see this sort of thing all the time. These girls feel anxious and nervous. They're flustered and freaked out; they're a bundle of nerves, a tangle of butterflies – they get themselves into a state and it's all to do with meeting YOU.

So, over to you guys. Are you brave enough to make an approach on the Frans, Alicias and Alisons of the world? Will you take a chance? If only on the basis that what doesn't kill you makes you stronger? Do you see that unless you chance it, the inevitable result is that there's this beyootiful woman sitting just over there, with buckets of romantic potential; this woman who could love you, yes YOU! But she's not flirting because she's shy and scared and nervous. So you don't go up to her because you're shy and scared and nervous. And it's all going to waste because neither of you know what the fuck you're doing!

### *Debate: Should Women Approach Men?*

Let's face it, traditionally, genetically, historically, just like every fairytale every told, women see their role as dishing out the signals and sitting back and waiting for *you to follow up.* You can say it's not right. You can say it doesn't make sense. You can say what I've said over and over again, *"It's not the 1950s – what's the freakin' problem?"*

But for the moment at least, the problem isn't going away. Though I'm working on it. I'm begging women to default to a smiley face and drop their defences. They've said they'll give it her best shot and I believe them. In the meanwhile there are exceptions to the rule, and if you are lucky enough to get approached by a girl you fancy – don't let her out of your sight!

How you would feel if a woman approached you? Pretty good 'eh? If you have been lucky enough to be approached, then well done you. Might I remind you that during these auspicious occasions you should never be rude or brusque to anyone, even if they're not your type. It's called dating karma so be nice. I don't care if she's got a head like a hairy football.

Likewise if you've never been approached, don't stress. Most women view this as something so truly out of their comfort zone; so remote from their beliefs, values and ideals – that it will most likely never happen. I can only empathise and say, I wish it was different. But it's not. And I'm sorry, but somebody's going to have to change or nothing's going to happen. Ever! So may the force be with you, and if that doesn't work, turn it off and turn it on again.

### New Kid On The Kop

Now that you are set to become king of the dating world, ask yourself how far you are prepared to go. What new approaches and techniques you will try? How will you open up new flirting opportunities? What steps will you take to make this part of your day-to-day life? Who can you start practising on? Lastly, are you prepared to go out on a limb and do whatever it takes to get a result?

If the answer is a high-fivin' *YES!* And you can you see yourself becoming more social, smiling more, making better eye-contact and generally not being such a sad bastard, then it goes without saying that soon you will look back on those dark days when you were to chicken shit to give this dating lark a go, and know that from hereon in, it's all about GOING FOR IT. Now grab a pen and notepad and complete the following:

*Describe your ideal Flirt Personality e.g.:* "I want to be more confident around women. I'd like to be dating as well. Once I'm kicking some goals, I'll feel more gung-ho."

*How will you open up new flirting opportunities?* I'll try talking to new people for starters. Usually when I go out with my mates, we don't talk to anyone else!

*Who can you start practising on?* There's plenty of girls at work and at the gym - so probably right in front of my nose...

*What will you do to get a result?* There are opportunities for me to do new stuff in my free time, it's just a matter of pulling my finger out and getting organised!

*What can you do immediately to become more interactive?* "Go to more new places. I've never been to a quiz night, so I'm going to try one."

66

## To summarise let's look at the Key Points

The key components of flirting are: body language, eye-contact and banter combined with the ABC's: Approachable, Bulletproof, Confident!

*In a Nutshell?* Your combined use of eye-contact, body language and banter will give you the momentum to kick-start your romantic exploits.

## Challenges

✓  Look, Listen and Learn
✓  Watch for signals
✓  Don't talk yourself out of anything!

## KPIs

*Once you've had a chance to get 'out there' you'll need to assess your progress:*

✓  Do you feel confident about your eye-contact?
   (Y/N)
✓  Are you getting better at reading women's body language?
   (Y/N)
✓  Have you picked up anything new by reading body language signals so far? (Y/N)
✓  Are you becoming more aware of how you come across to the ladies?
   (Y/N)
✓  Are you able to convey the 3 Cs: Confidence. Cheekiness. Charm?
   (Y/N)

***Mantra: If you're in a hole. Stop digging!***

If you've still got your 'L' Plates on and it all goes pear shaped, just remember your fallback Mantra: *I am Worthy! I am Hot! I am King of the Effing Universe!*

### *Checklist*

✓ *Attention to detail*

✓ *Consistency*

✓ *Confidence*

### *Little bag of tricks*

✓ *Business card*

✓ *Tic tics/gum/mints*

✓ *Camera-phone – because a well-timed happy-snap could close the deal!*

# Q & A

*What if I fancy someone who is way too good looking and out of my league?*

If you think she's out of your league, and you don't stand a chance, then I'm sorry, but right there, you've lost. That's because you don't have the confidence going in. In order to get it, you need to change your mindset good and proper. Because, in spite of what you might think, women aren't always so hung up on looks, and for that reason alone, it's worth having a go. You don't know what her type is, and who knows, it could be your lucky day. Just don't get your hopes up too high. And don't go home and kick the cat if it doesn't go as planned.

*I met a girl through a friend of a friend. We hit it off straight away. The thing is she's super friendly and really playful and she does that thing where she's always touching my arm when she's talking to me, but she does it with everyone else as well. How can I tell if it means anything?*

Two words: common sense. If she gives you a playful punch in the arm, or a pat on the hand – then that's pretty innocent, so you need to be on the lookout for other signals that will give it away. Is she doing it with a come-hither look while she juts her chest out? Is she flicking her hair and acting all girly and coy? If she's not doing any such thing, and she's just giving you a playful pat or punch without the other signals, then you can't read much into it beyond her being friendly. On the other hand, if she lets her hand languish on your leg, then it's a fair bet that she's trying to tell you something, so pay attention!

*There's a woman I met at work, we get along great and often have coffees and breaks together. I'd like to ask her out but...what to do if I think she likes me, but I'm not sure?*

Give her benefit of the doubt. Generally if we get the impression that someone likes us, then they probably do. Once you've cottoned on, just be enthusiastic. Let her know you enjoy her company. Just come right out and say it. *"You're funny!"* And how hard is it to say, *"You know what? We should do this outside of work"*. Practice saying these things in platonic situations where it doesn't count romantically. That way you'll find it much easier to say when it does count. Be cool, consistent and above all, be yourself! If she likes you she'll probably be passing on snippets about you to friends, so give her something to talk about!

# Step 2. Talking the Talk

# It's Not The Sausage, It's The Sizzle

The power of sex appeal isn't just about the way you look you know, women are looking for the full package. It's the tone of your voice, the twinkle in your eye, the extra little bit of 'sparkle'. It's not what you say, but *how you say it*. We're looking for good energy, a hint of reckless folly. So c'mon! Show us your mettle.

You'll know you've got it right, because all of a sudden when you speak, people listen, especially if you express yourself confidently. And by confidently, I don't mean waltzing over wearing a big grin and your, *'I'm So F\*\*\*in' Hot'* T-Shirt.

Funnily enough, chatting to women gets a whole lot easier when you've actually got something worth talking about. Especially when you're doing loads of interesting things that you can bang on about enthusiastically. Even better if you can link it up with your snappy up-to-date knowledge of what's going on in the world. Luckily for you, you'll find hundreds of suggestions in Step 5 to get you schmoozing, boozing, charming and seducing.

The guy who can causally mention the band, the book or the confused kitty he rescued – anything quirky at all, is the guy who has a much greater chance of hitting the Jackpot Moment. That's where the two of you bond over your shared enthusiasm of...well....anything really. Let's say the topic is holiday spots. You tell her you're just back from a mini-break in Outer Mongolia and ask if she has any holiday plans. She says, *'OMG, Outer Mongolia? That's my favourite holiday place!'* You punch the air with your fist: *'Yess!'* Things are always easy to convert into crackling sound-bites when they genuinely mean something to you.

The trick is to stop operating from the back-stalls and tear yourself away from whatever it is that's holding you back. Make a vow to get out of your room, out of the gloom and into the real world, where you become momentarily intrigued by, oh I don't know, the forgotten art of face-to-face conversation! It's called chatting and it's crucial to your tool-kit. You may be good at texting, tweeting, twittering and twaddling, but it's not much good if you can't hold a conversation! While we're on the subject, if your phone stresses you out with a constant stream of text, email and twitter, turn it off! Be gone ye textual predators.

### *Fancy Schmancy Words*

I'm not saying you need to be a walking, talking dictionary, or that you need be like those maddening people that talk in *italics* all the time, and bore us with relentless stories that go on and on and on. Nor do you need to cultivate conversation worthy of the Oxford Debating Team – you just need to tell us about fun stuff you've been doing. That's where your imagination kicks in, and you weave your story-telling magic with the mundane day-to-day. That means your version of last night's pizza delivery that went AWOL should be as compelling as an Agatha Christie mystery.

The good news is you can practice on anyone, anywhere, anytime. Ditch your play-it-cool mantra and spark up conversations from scratch. Sharpen up your act and practice with anyone and everyone from colleagues, cocktail waitresses and cabbies. Ease your way in by practicing on little old ladies. They tend to love a good ole chat, especially if they don't get many people to talk to, so you'll be doing a random act of kindness as well. There's no time to feel silly when all you're doing is communicating effectively. Loosen up, concentrate on the chitchat, listen hard and get those points ticking on the flirt-o-meter! Try a few different openers and make them your signature when it comes to jump-starting a conversation. Once you get the hang of it, your confidence levels will go berserk. Then you'll be ready to graduate to the hot babes.

Kick-start the process by rating your social skills. Is your banter is full of beans when you're with best buddies, but as flat as warm beer the minute you meet new people? If so, you need to sort it out. We can't have you turning into a quivering mess unable to cope with making small talk, or worse still, have you lapsing into awkward pauses peppered with '*ums and ahhs*' when the nerves kick in.

You're only human so you've no doubt experienced the nerve-wracking challenge of trying to hold a decent conversation with someone you really fancy, only to have that moment kick in when your mouth dries up, the words get stuck in your throat and you forget all the punch lines. The moment our HBA, *Hot Babe Alert* goes off we are struck down with the disease known scientifically as the 'Heebie-Jeebies'. More commonly known as: *"I like you and therefore – I have no idea what the fuck to say!"* Why is it so? It's *Sod's Law!*

Don't get me wrong, this ailment isn't restricted to men, women get struck down by it just as badly, all the time. The only cure, and the one I prescribe time and time again, is practice! That way you're less likely to be shaking in your boots, obsessing about, *'How hot she is'*. That'll only turn you into Nervous Nigel, and we can't be having that! Even if you are feeling jittery or uncomfortable, the only mistake you can truly make is to hold back for fear of making a twat of yourself. The problem with holding back, is that she'll never get to know the real you, especially if you go around imitating the sort of man you *think* she will like. She'll see straight through it. If you can manage to be relaxed and natural, and let words leap off the tongue, she'll see the essence of you – that's what we're talking about.

Of course random conversations will seem awkward if you're not used to them, hence why you need to get out there and start talking to new people. The trick is to use this as a test run for that OMG! Moment. Practice when it doesn't count, so that when you find yourself face to face with Missus-Oh-My-Freakin-God, you'll be ready and armed. *You'll be on fire!*

It's not just your social life that will benefit from your new skills, other areas will flourish as well. Having the gift of the gab will have a phenomenal effect on *all* the things you want out of life. Don't underestimate the power your conversational cunning has when it comes to catapulting your career, as well as your love life. How do you think the world's most successful entrepreneurs shot into the business stratosphere? It was largely thanks to their ability to thrive on a big personality, spin a yarn and above all party like it was 1999!

Lose the negative outlook as well. You may be tempted to whine about your boss, your sodding cow of an ex, or something equally dull, but please, try to refrain; we don't need to know. It's your spark and humour that conspires to catch our interest. Focus on the positives – always. Your goal is to be sharp, self-depreciative and witty as all hell! Get the girl to laugh at your jokes and then laugh some more, and you'll be in like Flynn!

## Hats Off To... *Public Speaking*

How would you describe your public speaking skills? If you're like the major population of Britons, they're likely to be pretty average. That's because millions of us are absolutely terrified of speaking in public, and the fear can be crippling. Yet it's something we're called upon to do almost every day in some format or another. Of course it's always going to be easier when it's informal with our mates, or colleagues, than when we feel put on the spot with hot babes – that's typically when we get all tongue-tied isn't it?

It goes without saying that if you clam up when you're put on the spot, whether it's in the boardroom or at the pub, then you will miss out on loads of opportunities. But if you can kill the nerves, you'll find that across the board, you will become better equipped to banter with strangers – which will of course lead to the bedroom. All I'm saying is that every little bit helps!

The good news is there are a million and one ways to fine-tune these skills from instructional books and videos to all kinds of courses in story-telling. It's not one of those things that you need to be born with, you can learn it. Once you've learnt it, it's a skill that you can use in any situation, and, you've got it for life.

So if you find the company of strangers still gives you verbal diarrhoea and your repartee isn't as good as it could be, don't let it be your Achilles heel, summon in the professionals and sharpen it up!

## Become a Communicator Extraordinaire

✓ Enrol for a debating group

✓ Sign up for Toastmasters and get to perform in a public forum

✓ Read *'How to Talk to Anyone'* by Leil Lowndes.

✓ Sign up for a Speed-dating session. More about this in Step 6.

✓ Learn Stand-Up comedy!

---

### Fact of the Day

*Less than a week after he was out of office, former PM Gordon Brown presented a talk for media students at a London college. As part of the Q & A session he told them that if he could do it all again, he would go back to Office equipped with PR and media skills. Because without them, he implied, you're screwed. You're telling us! That distorted smile and the flailing try hard gestures he used to illustrate his speeches completely missed the spot. If only he had been himself we sighed. Too late now!*

# Don't Get Mad, Get Funny!

In this, the age of war, recession and world-wide carnage, comedy is having its moment in the sun. It's the most popular and escapist form of entertainment around. There's nothing like it to escape the blues. It's one thing to watch it, but if you're game to give it a go yourself, performing your own stand-up comedy will have you leaping right out of your own skin. That's my cue for a story...

I embarked on my own stand-up comedy adventure in 2009. I'm here to tell you it was one of the hardest things I have ever done. I found it much harder than any day job; well I've never had a day job that depended on acting like a git to make people laugh! On the other hand, if I wanted to show off, or manipulate the audience, and say and do silly things in the name of entertainment – I'd come to the right place. It was pretty clear that I was in the midst of a huge learning curve, and considering the work I do, I need every communication skill I can get. Now that I've got the hang of it, I can honestly say that it's the best thing I've ever done. There are so many reasons I hardly know where to start.

On a social level alone, it expanded my network out of sight and introduced me to some of the best and funniest people I've ever met. From a self-confidence perspective, it's forced me to rethink the way I project and put things 'out there'. From a writing point of view, it has enabled me to develop a whole new approach to the way I look at situations and convert them into words. I've also learnt that it's possible to put a humorous spin on almost anything.

But boy oh boy, did I encounter some hiccups at the beginning! Not the least because the nature of my routine: all things mating, dating and matchmaking, meant that I didn't always have the women onside, presumably because they were with their boyfriends and feeling a bit touchy about the territory. On top of that, it took me a long time to find my comedy 'voice'. For the first twelve months I got up there and talked about everything except myself. I hid behind the one-liners and an encyclopaedic knowledge of pop culture. It was only when I did a course in stand-up, that my tutor, a lovely man called Keith, pulled me up on it.

'*The problem*', he said, was that I wasn't 'revealing' anything about myself. It was like I had something to hide. *"Who are you Sue?"* he asked one day after class. That's when I had the *aha!* moment. I was so intent on being 'clever' up there, that I'd missed the most obvious thing. That's when I changed everything.

After much tweaking and trialling different things, I turned my set on its head, and the central theme became all about me. I poked fun at myself relentlessly: my hair, make-up, star-sign, job, boyfriend – everything. I just went for it. Before I knew it, I started to win the audiences over – both sexes. Mind you it took a while, a lot longer than I ever imagined, but the rewards were fantastic. If I never I knew the meaning of the expression – you've got to fail in order to succeed – I knew it now. I absolutely fell on my arse, and not one time or two times, but loads of times. And the worse it was, the more determined I became. I don't like failing, or flailing in this case, and being the most stubborn person on the planet means I will put myself through almost anything in order to succeed. The best thing to come out of it was that nothing fazes me now. Seriously.

The other interesting thing I noticed, was the parallel between what I'm asking you to do – to get out of your comfort zone – and what I went through with the comedy. It's uncanny. Especially because I was working hard on this book the whole time I was gigging. The more I thought about it, the more I realised I would have never got on top of stand-up if I hadn't gone out and experienced it live in the real world: on a real stage, in a real pub, at a real gig in front of a real audience, every week for a the best part of a year. Falling flat on my face and underwhelming the audience was just part of it. I had to go through that to get to where I needed to go. That was my apprenticeship. I had to practice. I had to be brave. I had to take it on the chin. And so do you.

If you decide to try your hand at stand-up, then bravo, I applaud you in advance. And I'll tell you right now, two things will soon be evident. Firstly you will conquer the worst of your nerves, and your confidence will go through the roof. Secondly you will make a great impression on the ladies!

So, if you're intrigued and want to find out more, a good starting point is to check your local comedy venues and get along to any Open Mic night to see the amateurs in action. Then, if you like what you see and you've not done anything like it before, why not try a comedy course? I've made my recommendation at the end of this section for those readers in London, but otherwise, all cities offer them. And don't despair if carrying on like a git on stage isn't your thing, you can get your comic creative juices flowing in other ways – write a comedy rap instead. A very good mate of mine does and the girls love it!

***Recommended Stand-Up Comedy Course:***
*The Comedy School London http://thecomedyschool.com*

Q. Who said: "Laughter never goes out of fashion. It's like magic; it can get you anything – money, women, houses, cars, anything."

A. Seinfeld!

## They Say That Listening Is The Sexiest...

We've talked a lot about having the gift of the gab and how important that is, but I also want to celebrate that altogether more rare ability which is to *listen*. They say that men with the ability to listen are the sexiest people alive. Why? Because it lets the lady do what the lady wants to do. Do you know how sexy it is to tell us all yourself and your interests? *Not as sexy as if you just shut up and listen.*

Personally I know a whole lot of men who swear that during a first date they will do nothing but listen, nod, murmur, laugh ask questions, show an interest and without fail, end up in bed with the lady – I'm not saying that that need be the goal – just telling it how it is. Rule of thumb: nothing says *I want you and I want you now* like the man who can listen!

Often the things we recall from conversations are those things we reveal about ourselves in response to unexpected or quirky questions. So, rather than being on autopilot and fast-forwarding to what you will say next – or worse, going on and on about yourself since woman can't stand a show-off – make an effort to really stop and listen. Let the conversation follow its natural course and take the time to respond thoughtfully. Pepper the exchange with light-hearted questions, and don't whatever you do, stick to a script. You're not on a fact finding mission. You can find out all the facts in the world later, *if* there's any chemistry. First you need to make a connection.

The aim is to make someone feel special and put them in the spotlight. So don't be looking over her shoulder or craning your head to see who's 'over there'. The message should be: *'It's all about you!'* Look her squarely in the eye, pay attention and indulge her Princess Syndrome. If she wants to talk about Vegan Junk Food, talk about Vegan Junk Food. Just do whatever it takes to make her feel like the Only Girl in the World.

*Case Study: No-one was surprised when Jacqui walked away with the Best and Fairest Flirt Award that freezing night in February. The difference in her from the beginning to end of the night was startling. She was a natural, but, she was also very self-conscious.*

*After a pep-talk the night kicked into action and by the time we sashayed into a boisterous Bloomsbury boozer, Jacqui was on fire, bewitching every guy that came near her.*

*I watched closely to see what her secret was. Her biggest strength was that she was a really good listener. NO-ONE can resist a great listener, and somehow, every good flirt knows how to listen instinctively. Jacqui asked lots of questions and she listened to the answers. She kept the conversation going and she kept it light and breezy.*

*If you see a gorgeous girl flexing her listening muscle, cocking her head, listening intently, using her eyes – you gotta know that she's flirting with you!*

## Hang About, What Is Charm?

Let's start with what is charm is not. Charm is not the bullocks that the pick-up artists and the players dish out – those to whom every cheesy one-liner is clearly rehearsed. Charm is not the dodgy dude who talks only in clichés and cheap innuendo, and thinks all women are desperate morons there to be poked and prodded expressly for his pleasure. Charm is not the dapper chappy who slathers on the compliments as thickly and slickly as an oil-well. Nor is Charm those cheeky Charity Workers who leap all over you like excitable puppies whenever you walk down any street in Central London. No, that is not charm.

Charm is spontaneous and real. It's the off the cuff compliment you didn't see coming; the interest from someone who is genuinely interested in YOU and how you're going. Charm is a warm, happy fellow human being who loves your company, and isn't afraid to let you know. Charm is when someone you barely know makes you feel ten foot tall.

That is charm.

On a practical level, charm is ignited by an interaction; it's what happens when you access someone's world, and link it in with yours. It's that moment during a conversation when you acknowledge and pick up on someone's innate thoughts, their dreams, fears and passions, and bring the topic around to *their* world – to the things *they're* into. So if I was talking to you about a film, a book or a band that I enjoyed, and I said, *"YOU would love it!"* That's charm right there. All you need to remember about charm is that it's all about THEM. If you can remember that, you'll do just fine.

*Bottom line:* if you're not a trust-fund baby or the descendant of an Indian sultan, and all the riches that incorporates, you'll need to flex that charm muscle and be on the charm offensive 24/7! *Shizzle ma nizzle!*

## Mind The Gap

Here in Britain it is deemed impolite to have even the tiniest pause between conversational patter. But rather than fear it, why not look at it another way? The pause provides a chance to see *where the other person will take things.* If you insist on controlling the whole kit and caboodle, or if you pride yourself on your very ability to do so, and many do, it's not going to deliver any surprises. But if you let it career on its own for a bit, and venture right into those mysterious nooks and crannies – you might come out of it with more than you expected – the top shelf stuff.

The trick is not to get all panicky and freak-out if there is a moment's gap in your banter. Silence *is not the enemy.* Rather than fretting, better to follow the simple rules of body language and fill in the gaps with lots of reassuring eye-contact and responsive smiles and nods. These are the non-verbal signs that show you're paying attention. Go for quality over quantity, and have faith that the conversation will take care of itself, provided you're both into it. The silence doesn't have to be awkward. It can be peaceful and amicable. A way to show you're comfortable with each other. If there really is nothing else to talk about, just ask about her favourite subject – herself – you cannot fail! Otherwise if have no option but to talk about the dreaded weather, at least do it with an ironic wink.

## Watchdog Lookout: Interupt-itis

Don't interrupt already! Why do guys have a habit of jumping in to the conversation with the old, *'Been there! Done that!'* Of course it's fine to interject, but wait until she's finished before barging in with your version halfway through. Let her get to the end of her story first *and then* dazzle her with yours; even if you think yours is more interesting! Likewise, wait until the time is right to reveal a tit-bit about yourself, before flipping the spotlight back to her. Keep the chat well balanced whilst encouraging her to open up.

- ✘ *Don't ask questions and then talk all over the answer*

- ✘ *Don't look over her shoulder, or swivel your head around*

- ✘ *Don't fast forward to what you'll say next – wait for her to finish*

- ✘ *Don't try to impress with your story which is bigger, better and funnier – at least until she's finished*

# Don't Apologise, Don't Explain

Most of the consultations I do take place across Central London in various cafes and bars where I am meeting people for the first time. Part of my job is to assess them from the minute I set eyes on them. And whilst body language and eye-contact conveys one thing, I'm usually struck by what they say. Often they will apologise, for no good reason, except it seems, to fill in a gap. They'll apologise because they didn't spot me straight away. They'll apologise for not heading straight to where I was sitting. They'll apologise because they didn't bring the right money – there's too much apologising! Of course I appreciate manners but there are alternative ways to acknowledge a situation without apologising all the time. It sets a bad precedent. Apologising without good reason should be against the law.

***Bloke Quote:*** *"I don't like liars, I don't like cheats. I don't like bullshitters. I don't like schmoozers. I don't like arse-lickers."*

– Lord Alan Sugar

### *International Men of Mystery Don't Tell All Their Secrets!*

Avoid the case of 'too much, too soon'. Revealing all your dark secrets too early is a big no-no! By all means have a laugh at your own expense, but don't go overboard. She doesn't have to know the gory details about:

✗ *Your rug of back hair*

✗ *What you ate in China that time*

✗ *What happened behind the shelter sheds*

✗ *That you wax your… whatever*

✓ TMI: Too much information!

### *Lost in Translation*

Sometimes the most important things get lost in translation. One minute you're having a great old chat and the next, your lady-friend throws in something random, and you know it's cheeky because she's definitely got that glint in her eye, but you don't quite get the gist of it, so rather than ask her to repeat it, or expand, you just smile and nod and ignore it like the great git that you are! That leads to a massive miscommunication where she's left feeling deflated because she had hoped to set things off in a more intimate direction and get to know you a little better. Instead she's feels like it's Game Over.

Moral of the Story: when in doubt, ASK!

Sometimes the most important things get lost in translation. One minute you're having a great old chat, and then the next, your lady-friend throws in something a little cheeky, but, if you don't quite understand what she's getting at, you may not stop to ask her to repeat it, or expand – you just smile and nod and ignore it like the great git that you are! Which leads to a great big miscommunication where she's left feeling all deflated, because for all you know, she hoped to set things off in a more intimate direction and, you know, get to know you a little better. Now she's left feeling like it's Game Over.

Moral of the Story: when in doubt, ask!

*Case Study:* *Alexandria is one very sexy lady: all cheekbones, feline eyes and sleek body language; a lethal combination which conspires to say everything that words cannot. Especially when the challenge is her accent.*

*Alexandria is Russian, possibly one of the most glamorous women to come out of Russia. But, as sexy as her accent is, and it really is, she's very self conscious about it. As such she lacks the confidence to launch herself into conversations. The end result is that most of the time she's left waiting by the sidelines.*

*Alexandria wishes she could worry less about the language barrier and focus more on being playful, but because she feels self-conscious, she's not as outgoing as she would like to be. And to be honest, if you glimpsed her across the room, you would write her off as the Ice Queen – that's what we tend to think when we spot a six-foot svelte blonde who looks like a modern day Brigitte Nielsen – is it not? When the reality is that she feels socially awkward and in this case, it comes across as looking unfriendly, or at the very least, unapproachable.*

*Consider this: Would you make an approach on someone if they looked completely unapproachable? I'm assuming the answer is 'no!' If it is, you could be missing a trick, because in many cases, nothing could be further than the truth. Alexandria would be over the moon if you came over and introduced yourself, even if it's only the basis that nobody decent ever does! This is true of many beautiful women the world over. They don't get hit on enough because they're seen to be intimidating. Or they only get hit on from the players, not the genuine guys. So if you see a statuesque blonde in your midst, don't automatically assume she won't want to chat, just suck it and see.*

# Compliment-itis

Is it just me or have you noticed how no-one compliments anyone anymore? It's a dying art form. And since we rarely get compliments, we don't think to dish them out. A symptom of the crazily busy times we live in. In some cities people are just downright aggressive; pushing and shoving with barely a grunt of apology. That's the harsh reality of life in the big city. No-one has time for old-school manners. Everyone's too busy to stop and smile, or say hello. It's such a shame because a well-timed compliment can absolutely make someone's day. I find it so sad that no-one uses this simple and obvious way to connect. These days, pretty much the only regular compliments women can depend on for their ego fix, are from the building site workers who retreat to the safely of their mates amidst cries of: *"Oi, love, fancy one?"*

Surely I am not the only one longing for a glimpse back to a time where men would tip their hat, kiss a lady's hand, and dish out an elegant compliment *without the fear of getting bitch slapped*? I didn't think so. Nor am I the only one who's a sucker for old-fashion values – they rock! Generally speaking, women will applaud a man who acts in a gentlemanly way, whether he says something lovely, gestures for her to step ahead of him, or opens the door. For most of us, a juicy compliment truly makes our day, *"Great shoes. Great smile!"* Is all it takes! Having said that, you will occasionally encounter a grumpy bad apple here and there; but that's fine, so long as you don't let them spoil the bunch.

### *Brain teaser: Does the English Gent actually exist anymore?*

Compliments are the best ice-breakers and most of us will take them any way we can get them. But it's nice to hear those compliments we've not heard before. So when we hear the bog standard Mr Happy line trotted out: *"You've got beautiful legs/hair/breasticles."* It's a bit like, *"C'mon! Is that the best you got?!"* It's not like we go around peering at your wotsits and saying, *"Oi, nice package!"*

Try to be innovative with your compliments and think laterally. Compliment our, our.... shoes – there's a good one! Guys just don't comment on our shoes nearly enough, and god knows we spend half our salary on them. So if we're rocking a pair of shoes that scream, *'Don't mess with me'* and you're secretly thinking, *'Oh my lord, a more erotic pair of Eff-Me-Heels I have never seen'* you need to find a way to *tell us* our shoes are smoking. We will love you for it!

It's also lovely to receive compliments on accessories, but again, it's best to be specific. Put your observational super-seducer skills to the test and look out for the tiniest and most delicate of trinkets and charms and all sorts of spangly things. As soon as a girly touch catch your eye – a quirky hair slide, a pretty pair of earrings – let her know. She's gone out of her way to draw attention to herself so why not show her you appreciate that – even if it doesn't bling the house down.

We will also rate you highly if you notice the overall picture, or the whole *'look'*, rather than just one part. So rather than saying *'Nice dress!'* you might try, *'You look AMAZING in that dress.'* Or *'That dress really suits you.'* It's a subtle difference, but effective, especially when we've put in the effort. Try to tailor the compliment and personalise it:

✓  *That suit makes you look seriously good!*

✓  *That jacket – the colour and the cut - looks amazing on you!*

✓  *You've got the tiniest waist in that dress!*

✓  *The dress, the shoes, the pearls - you look beautiful!*

Let's see if you've got what it takes to applaud her efforts. Granted, part of our effort with the way we are turned out is designed to impress other women, but, if someone is spending time with you and she likes you, then either directly or indirectly, the way she is styled is in some ways, for your benefit. Of course the compliment doesn't have to be restricted to what she's wearing; in fact, you'll earn loads of brownie points if it's something unusual, or something she hasn't heard before. Anything like:

➤ You've got a real presence

➤ I like the way you think

➤ The world needs more people like you

➤ I feel like I've known you forever

➤ You remind me of a really close friend

➤ I noticed you when you walked in

## Accept That Compliment Damn You!

Until such time as you're ready to dish out the compliments face-to-face, the *Catch You Later* compliment is a nice way to ease in. Reserved for Flirts in Training, it allows you to dart up to someone, deposit a nice juicy compliment and dash off before they have a chance to reply. The benefits are plentiful. First you get to make someone's day (that's always nice). Second, you don't run the risk of rejection. Brilliant! Lastly it gives you the chance to practice your style when it doesn't count, so you'll be as smooth as silk when it does!

*Here's how it works:* Select your target and focus in on something – maybe it's a pair of shiny stilettos, a diamante TOYBOY belt, or an interesting piece of costume jewellery. It could be anything at all. Everyone's got something worth complimenting. You just have to look for it. And then, as you wander by, just smile and say it, whatever it is:

✓  *Love your bracelets!*

✓  *Great jacket!*

✓  *Cool shoes!*

Then, flash that smile and stride away. You don't have to stick around and wait for an answer. That's the point; she doesn't feel all awkward about what to say back. But, it gives her is a little something to think about later, hmmmm? And who knows, she may return the favour when she sees you next, so if nothing else, you've broken the ice. See if you can come up with 3 specific compliments based on those special women that you fancy or have fancied. Nothing naughty thanks folks!

➢  Jenny: beautiful eyes

➢  Amy: great hair and style

➢  Karen: a body to die for!

Practice your compliment prowess with everyone you see. Make a note of their best assets – keep it clean – try to find something great to say about everyone. Whether it's their sense of humour, banana peeling ability, hair, tan, teeth, skin, smile, shoes, freckles, hands, muscle tone, hip to waist ratio, little black dress, toes, fingers – anything, just look for the positives. Once you get into the swing of it and begin to appreciate the power behind the almighty compliment, you will be more likely to dish them out. Added bonus, once you feel courageous, you will be unstoppable.

### *Likewise when you get a compliment, you should NOT:*

➤ Tell them they must be BLIND!

➤ Ask them what their problem is

➤ Say can't we just cut to the chase already?

➤ Bore them with a lengthy explanation

➤  Scowl and say, *'Yeah rrrrright!!'*

### *Instead you could try:*

➤ It's my favourite too! I love it because…

➤ Ah yes, I got it while I was travelling in….

➤ You've made me feel ten foot tall!

➤ Mademoiselle, you make me blush at your delicious impudence.

➤  Thank you!

Let me interrupt myself for a minute. I've had my share of compliments, and I'm not complaining, I love them just as much as the next person, possibly even more! Ask me about my most memorable ones, and I'd have to say they're never the obvious ones, they're the quirky ones – that's what makes them special. The compliment I remember the most was about my 'character', which according to this one bloke, was the best he had ever come across. The appeal was simply that no-one else had ever said it. *'You've got a sexy face'* was another of my favourites!

# Questions, Ice-Breakers and Random Openers

Ice-breakers that fit the bill are usually the obvious ones. You're not looking for anything too flash. The best things to talk about are often right in front of you. You're looking to create a bond; the easiest way to do that is over your surrounds. You already have that in common since you're both at the same place at the same time, so use that! Be prepared to think on your feet and use your common sense. Choose material suited to the situation and aim to have some snappy ice-breakers at the ready. Have you thought it through? Where are your props? What's happening in the background? What have you prepared? What do you have up your sleeve?

Before we look at how to keep things ticking over, a Royal Fact...

Prince Philip, the Duke of Edinburgh, has stood at the Queen's side for nearly 60 years. He has become the longest serving consort in British history. His reluctance to speak about all aspects of his life is well documented and is, according to his son, Prince Edward and told to the BBC, due to modesty:

*"My father plain and simply is very modest about himself and doesn't believe in talking about himself. One of his best pieces of advice he gives to everybody is talk about everything else, don't talk about yourself - nobody's interested in you."*

And yet, in spite of the Prince's wise words, there is a whole world of dating advice that encourages you to ask questions relentlessly. The message is, so long as you're asking a woman's opinion on...well anything, you'll be fine. And I get that, but I also hear women's side of it. And here's what you need to know: often they complain that you guys are so busy with your persistent questions, that they don't get a chance to find out anything about you. You just can't win can you?!

If you're in a desperate race against time to find out everything about someone on the first meeting, may I suggest that you sit back and take a big breath instead. The trick is to take it easy. Otherwise she might feel

93

like she's being cross-examined, and no-one likes that[3]. Strive to find a balance between firing off questions and revealing titbits about yourself.

- ✓ Ask questions *without* interrogating – leave that to the women ☺
- ✓ Go on the charm offensive. Be interested and interesting.
- ✓ Make it worth her effort.

---

[3] It goes without saying that women can be very guilty of this – and you probably don't like it either!

### Hats Off To…Tag questions

You may already know about Tag Questions, perhaps you learnt the technique in primary school, but even if you did, you're likely to have forgotten since we rarely use them as adults, which is a shame because Tag Questions are an effective way to reveal some interesting things about yourself, whilst finding out lots of good stuff about somebody else. The idea is to open up a topic and reveal some tit-bit, and then throw it out into the open.

So instead of:

*"Do you work out?"*

You might say:

*"I don't work out as often as I'd like. But you're in amazing shape. What's your secret?"*

And then, I swear to god, watch as her whole face changes as she says:

*"Exercise! Every day I run for one hour! It is the only way to keep fit!"*

Likewise with:

*"Been on any good holidays lately?"*

Try:

*"I went to Ireland for NYE. I drank enough Guinness to sink a pirate ship. What's your best ever NYE?"*

### The Deep & Meaningful

Once you're chit-chatting away and it's all bells and whistles, you'll want to get the essence of this woman, and find out what she's all about. The best way of doing that is to delve into more personal territory once the conversation broadens out. Instead of asking the dreary questions, go one step further in a bid to tap into your playmate's psyche. If she mentions recent changes she's been through, either in her personal or professional life, ask how she's coping with the 'change', rather than just the bog standard, '*How's work?*' Or if there's a comparable experience that you can offer, like maybe you went through a massive career overhaul of your own recently, then put that out there.

*Question Time:* For conversations that flow like liquid sunshine, ask open-ended questions that can't be answered with a straight 'yes' or 'no'. There's nowhere to go when you get one word responses which usually happens when we say things like:

*"Great party huh?"*

And then you're left wondering what on earth to say when you get an answer like:

*"Yep!"*

Yet if you tried:

*"Great BBQ. How do you know our host?"*

And the answer is:

*"Alex and I went to high-school together."*

Then you've hit the jackpot! Now you've got a wealth of material to mine, so it's just a matter of continuing along in that direction.

Focus on the positives and ask questions which can glide down another intriguing path and hopefully end in a *Jackpot Moment*, that's what you're after, clues to keep things crackling along. Use questions based around the same theme: *Where did they grow up? What do they like best about the new place?* Once the conversation broadens out use the 'I' word as much as you like – just be sure it extends to include them:

*"I usually go out in North London. What's your favorite party area?"*

*"I just had my 35$^{th}$ birthday – big party! What about you? Any exciting birthday plans?"*

*"I usually get away hiking on the weekends..."*

*"I love going out for a roast on Sundays..."*

*"I tend to spend my Saturday nights..."*

### *Charge your glasses to…The Bleedin' Obvious*

More and more I hear stories from pro-active women who follow the basic rule that *'you never know where you'll meet someone';* as such they're open to the idea of meeting someone at the supermarket, or at a café. But even though they have the best intentions in the world, if they do spot a fanciable man, they tend to freeze in the heat of the moment, completely lose their nerve and not know what to say.

I should know because often they'll text me desperately wanting to know: *'What should I say? What should I do?'* My advice to the ladies is exactly the same as it is to YOU. Use your imagination, think on your feet. Find an opener to fit the surrounds and the setting. Say something, say anything! Just open your mouth and speak!!

Likewise next time you're out and about, in a shopping centre or at Lady Sat-alone Cafe and you see an opportunity, just start up a chat. I know you think it's weird, being British and all, but it's not *that* weird. Get over the idea that you'll come across all Uncle Purvey because you *oooh-er* spoke to a stranger. It's silly! The amount of opportunities you stand to lose because of your sodding pride isn't worth it! I have people come up to me all the time to start any old conversation. I don't have a problem with it, nor should you.

### *Rule of thumb*

➢ If you're at the bar, talk about the drinks!

➢ If you're at a gig, talk about the band!

➢ If you're at a coffee shop – talk about the coffee!

➢ If you're at the railroad, talk about the trains!

➢ If you're at the bus-stop, talk about the bus!

➢ If you're at the cab-rank, talk about the cabs!

### Backdrop and Location

*You're in the same place at the same time so you've already got your opener. Use that to get things started!*

### Last hurrahs at the bar: *Fancyadrinkthen?*

You're standing at the bar waiting to order when a hot damn! babe with a tempting grin pointed your way props up right next to you. With posture that would put Beckham to shame, you volley that smile right back and swing straight into it:

*"I'm taking a poll for the bar, which do you prefer:*

➢ Cocktails, Corona or Champagne?

➢ Beer, Bellinis or Bacardi?

➢ Shooters, Shots or Sangria?"

Likewise look at the props around you, if there's a pool table ask if she plays pool. If there's a jukebox, ask for her request. If there's a dance-floor, ask her to dance. Ask anything, just open your mouth. What's the worst thing that can happen if you ask:

➢ Do you know if it's still Happy Hour?

➢ Would you like a straw with that?

➢ Do you know what time they're open 'til?

➢ Do you know anywhere nearby to eat?

➢ Do you know anywhere to kick on afterwards?

By the time she's answered, you will have offered to buy her a drink, *of course you have.* And no doubt you used some variation of the following:

➢ *You look thirsty and I'm getting a drink; shall I get you one?*

➢ *You look like you could do with a Long Tall Glass of something fabulous. Fancy it?*

➢ *I'm not letting out of my sight until I've bought you a drink!*

### *At Starbucks:*

➢ *I see you're having the Vanilla-light-Grande-decaff-toffee-frappuchino – me too. That makes us coffee soul-mates!*

➢ *Can I ask about your laptop? (I get this all the time)*

➢ *May I borrow your copy of Time Out? (also popular)*

➢ *Could I borrow your pen?*

➢ *Does your phone have Bluetooth?*

➢ *Will you mind my things while I order a coffee? (I get this one all the time as well)*

➢ *Do you have a pen? (Ditto the above!)*

### *At the Gig:*

➢ *Do you know what time the band's on?*

➢ *Do you know who the support is?*

➢ *Do you know if the support's been on yet?*

➢ *Do you know who this band is?*

➢ *What's your favourite ever gig then?*

### At the Supermarket
This is a no-brainer. She's buying food. You're buying food...Use your imagination! *"So can I interest you in some English sausage?"* Kidding!!

### On the Street
➤ *You look smart today. Going anywhere nice?*

➤ *Excuse me could you tell me where you got the coffee/sandwich/drink/fill in the blank*

### On a Park Bench
*"Excuse me, I found this lighter, is it yours?"*

### Public Spaces: Sports Arenas/Tourist Spots//Restaurants/Hotels
*"Do you know if they have Wi-Fi?"*

### At a Shopping Centre
*"Do you know where I can find.. (*fill in the blank)"

### At the Library
*Stop Press:* Right now as I was hard at work at my local library, a chap came over and asked about the Wi-Fi: was it accessible? I told him it was and he dashed off. A moment or two later, he came back. This time he asked about my choice of printing paper – pink if you must know. And then he asked, wait for it, was I dyslexic? I looked at him a bit stunned. He explained that people with dyslexia read more effectively from coloured paper. The funny thing is, I actually am slightly dyslexic, so I was quite interested in what he had to say. Then he told me he was off the British Library but maybe he'd see me tomorrow and off he toddled. How funny!

Oh, and I always get asked about being left handed. Everyone's always got something to say about that. My favourite is, *"you wouldn't know your right mind."* Too right!

### Conversation Extenders

A personal favourite of mine which no-one ever asks, for reasons I don't understand, is any variation of the 'Highlight' Question. It's simple and deadly, and usually most effective with someone you know, even just a little bit.

✓ *"What was the best thing about your day/week/month/year?"*
   Or any variation on *'How's life?'*

✓ *"We've got so much to catch up on. What's been happening with you?"*
✓ *"It's been ages. What's been going on?"*
✓ *"You look fantastic! How have you been?"*

### Here's Proof: Asking the most obvious thing is the most effective

*True Story:* I was waiting for my train one wet and woeful Wednesday when I was hit on by a couple of Aussies. Their opener was: *"You are the hottest woman we've seen in London. You are truly stunning."* All right, then I made that up. What they really said was, *"Does this train go to Paddington?"* A straightforward question which invited a straightforward answer, but one that turned into a ten minute fun-filled banter. Evidence that all you need to do is try. Lose the fear and flirt anyway!

Often I'm asked, *'Yes, but what happens then?'* To which I say, play it by ear. If she's up for a chat, great! If not, too bad. The goal isn't to marry her. It's merely to practice. If you manage to get a number (or a date) out of it, then well done you! If not, you know the drill, get on the bus Gus!

### *Dating IQ…What NOT To Use as an Opener*

Anything that starts with *'Have you ever had a full lesbian experience…?'* is guaranteed to get her attention, but may not get the response you were hoping for! Definitely preferable to start with a low-fi approach. And if things do take off, don't lose your nerve and go into excruciating detail about your phone plan, card tricks, skate-board techniques, Dungeons & Dragons, or how you fixed your computer – we don't care! Do however go into detail about the trip you took into the forest to chop down wood for your log fire, we'll be impressed. Even better if you can casually manage an invite where you will casually split said log in half and stoke the fire, in our presence. *That'll do it!*

# Yes, But What Do I Say?

If your ice-breaker takes you through to second base and she's keen to hang about, then great, so far, so fabulous; now you just have to keep her interest. And then, it happens; after a promising start, all high energy and seductive smiles, you can't think of a damn thing to say! So what do you say? How about we look at what *not* to say, like asking the tragically predictable: *"So, what do you do?"*

I know it's a social norm but, I'm sorry, it's the biggest conversation killer of all. This is a social occasion and it's meant to be fun – *don't make it all about work!* It doesn't matter how much you love your job, or how much she loves hers, you're not there to recite your CV, or bang on and on about the day-job. Whether we realise it or not, we do go to a weird place when we talk about our jobs, and without realising we revert back to our 9-5 selves, which is a pretty good way to yank anybody right out of the seduction setting! You could argue that women are extremely interested in what you do, and I accept that. And maybe you think your profession is your biggest draw card, but I would argue that no matter how sexy your job, you're always better off to play it down and stick to general topics. I personally think there's something way cool about guys who do impressive jobs for a living but don't go on and on about them. By all means tell the lady what you do and enquire as to what she does, but then get the job thing out of the way and switch the subject to something FUN. Find that common ground if it's the last thing you do. And if it turns out that it's work related, that's OK, just try not to let it take over the entire conversation.

### *What's She Listening for? She'll know you're keen if you:*

➢   Use her name regularly

➢   Tell her about something fun you're doing tomorrow night

➢   Talk about the bands, movies or restaurants you'd like to check out

➢   Make an effort to talk (not flirt) with her buddies

- ➢ Offer to buy her a drink
- ➢ Tell her that being single is great, but…
- ➢ Give her your phone number
- ➢ Ask for her phone number
- ➢ Compliment her – on anything at all

### Who's the Donkey? Have A Stash of 'I'm Such a Git Stories'

Anyone who can have a laugh at their own expense is irresistible. It shows a hint of vulnerability and self-depreciation which according to recent British studies is a crucial key to seduction. Indeed, our own Russell Brand is the master. So you're not perfect 'eh? Who would've known? Package it up and put it out there. You'll get ten points for every conversational nugget you whip out that's even mildly embarrassing.

### Right then, off you go…

- ➢ *I was such a git to my boss today*
- ➢ *I was such a git to my little brother*
- ➢ *I was such a git to my mum*
- ➢ *I was such a git to the bouncer*
- ➢ *I was such a git to the parking cop*
- ➢ *I was such a git to the police*

### More Git Fun...

- ➢ *I realised I had mismatched shoes on – after I left home today!*
- ➢ *I ate Garlic Prawns for lunch today. Ooops!*
- ➢ *Apologies in advance for my appearance. I forgot to shave for the past 3 months!*

106

### *Name Game: What's My Name?*

Making a conscious decision to remember names is pretty basic stuff, but surprisingly few people actually do it. Using this mnemonics technique will help.

Once you've been introduced to someone, stop for a second and look them in the eye while you *absorb their name.* Then think of someone else you know with that name, visualise them, and link the two names together, saying it to yourself three times. If you don't know anyone with the same name, use an object or a rhyme, or a rude word if it takes your fancy. So if her name is 'Anita', she becomes 'All Nighter' while Jen becomes 'Gem'. It might seem silly but it works. Apply this technique to facts and information as well by using funny images as mental reminders. Take pride in your ability to remember names, faces and facts and you'll stand out in the crowd because you may well be the only one who's bothered!

***But wait, how are you going on the Personality Scale? Have you:***

✓ *Made her laugh?*

✓ *Ordered the drinks?*

✓ *Asked lots of questions?*

✓ *Listened for the answers?*

✓ *Carried your share of the conversation?*

✓ *Kept your facial expression tuned to 'interested!'*

Of course there will be days you don't feel like flirting, but do it anyway and just see how you go. You might be surprised how much better you feel once it clicks in. If it doesn't, you don't have to beat yourself up about it. Just go home and read a good book, preferably mine.

# Dodgy Pick-up Lines

Now that we've considered the thinking man's approach and looked at the good stuff, the wise and witty openers and ice-breakers *that do work*, let's look at the really bad stuff.

Don't even think about stepping out with a fistful of woeful pick-up lines, because make no mistake mister, *you will go down.* Over the years I've surveyed thousands of women who overwhelmingly agree that pick-up lines are the lowest of the low. Some things just won't cut it and I'm afraid this is one of them.. It doesn't matter how clever or original you think they are, they will come across for exactly what they are, second-hand one-liners, and nine times out of ten, they will go horribly, tragically wrong, and you will get the silent treatment, or maybe even a *slap* because sadly for you, she's not stupid, and she won't fall for it.

On top of that, you'll be so anxious about how to manage the delivery of your crappy one-liner that you'll screw it up anyway. Or, if you do mange to raise a laugh, it's because you're a brilliantly gifted comedian; or we're absolutely stonkered – either way, it's a short lived victory. If you still choose to go ahead, don't say you weren't warned!

The same goes if you approach a woman with all your swagger, bravado and charm, and dish out phoney compliments like they're mints, *she will smell a rat.* She'll also figure if you're like that with her, you're doing the same with every hot babe you meet along the way. So if you vow to wow with a fake brand of showmanship, all I can say is – don't. You're only kidding yourself.

The point is to be YOURSELF. You don't have to pile it on to impress us, because it's not about that. If we get the ESSENCE of you and we like it – we will like you. It's that simple. We just need to see beyond the bullshit.

## *Negging*

Are you familiar with this 'negging' business? It's a reverse psychology gimmick that says men should pay women a backhanded compliment so that she feels insecure and turns her full attention on the bloke in a bid to win back his affections, sort of like begging for approval. Say the bloke says: *'I like your nails. Are they false?* The woman is supposed to drop to her knees and plead for his attention. Brilliant isn't it? The thing is women are awake up to this bizarre practice. That's why it doesn't work, not on sassy women anyway.

The practice of negging only serves to make women feel intimidated and awful, and nine times out of ten, they will just want to get away as fast as possible. Anyway, what kind of loser can't genuinely compliment a woman for god's sake? Is it really that hard that you have to make the girl cry before you make a move on her? Of course if you pick on the most insecure woman in the world, it might work. Otherwise you'll just remind us of the school-yard bully. It's the same kind of mentality isn't it? Where little boys pulled little girls pigtails to make us cry and then tried to kiss us! Seriously, whichever way you look at it, dreary chat-up lines and silly mind-games are not the way forward.

### *Word of Warning: don't try any of the following!*

✗ *I love you in that outfit. You look like an expensive hooker. (Ouch!)*

✗ *I'm gonna' keep drinking while you still look good.(WTF?!)*

✗ *I like your friend, is she coming tonight? (Slap)*

✗ *I love your lipstick. Especially the way you wear it on your teeth.(Back off!)*

✗ *You look amazing since you lost weight (Watch it Bozo)*

### The Good, The Bad and The Ugly

There is no such thing as a good pick up line, and while some of them are so bad they're hilarious, others border on the sublimely ridiculous:

➤ *I love that star shaped ring; it reminds me of the stars in your eyes. (Ewgh!)*

➤ *I like your belt. (Where do you go from there!?)*

➤ *I love the way you look in that top (Erm)*

➤ *Are you a model? (You're kidding right!!)*

➤ *What's your favourite side of the bed? (Huh?)*

➤ *You look like the twin of the woman who broke my heart (Puke!)*

➤ *I like your legs, what time do they open for business? (WT..?)*

### At a pinch, you might get away with:

➤ *You've got the best laugh I ever heard! (Excellent!)*

➤ *I could listen to you talk all night long (Nice!)*

➤ *Your arms are so toned, you must work out! (Good)*

➤ *Are we flirting yet? (Straight out of the Russell Brand school of flirting)*

➤ *You ask her 'what do you call a karate kickin' pig.*

*She says: `A Pork Chop!' And bam, you're in!*

## Mixed Wires

You know that feeling, when there's someone you don't know very well, but you fancy them and from there it's all downhill. The nerves kick in, you feel weird, you can't think of a thing to say and you seem to constantly shoot yourself in the foot. Here's a real life example from someone, let's call her Kate, because that's her name, about her experience. One spring day she was sitting looking really nice and perky, when this bozzo (her term) comes up to her and says:

*"Will you do just one thing for me? SMILE!"*

Her response was to give him an icy glare (her usual angry pout) and respond with:

*"I only smile when I find something amusing to smile about. Your pathetic comedic attempt is funny in a tedious way, but not THAT funny".*

*Ouch!*

But the problem, she admitted afterwards, was that even though she *actually liked him*, she had no way of letting him know after he blew it with his too-cool-for-school opener.

*"Sure I fancy him, but he pissed me off"* she said, *"So where did that leave me?"*

The moral of the story is that being a feisty woman and all, she would rather miss out, than let him get away with being cocky. Why? Female Pride, why else!

But what did he *do* that was so wrong? It's just like she said – his attempt at humour was right off the mark, it just killed it for her. 'Bozzo' needed to think it through first and try something that was going to work with Kate's prickly personality. There are too many conversation killers which have exactly the same effect.

111

Take the line:

*"I may not be Barney Rubble, but I'll bet I know how to make your bed rock"*

May raise a chuckle, but where do you go from there?!

Likewise:

*"I want to discover everything about you right from when you were a little girl.* (Please. You don't even know me).

*Or,*

*"I forgot my phone number, can I have yours?* (Ever so cheesy but if you've got a GSOH you might get away with it)

*Or,*

*"You're the most beautiful girl in the room tonight"* (At which point she immediately turns to count how many women there are in the room)

*Or,*

*You remind me of a young ...."* (Insert token movie star) It's cringeful when you know you don't really look like Kate Moss!)

Plus a billion variations in-between.

The outcome is always the same, there's that awkward eye-rolling moment where she bites her tongue because she doesn't necessarily want to tell you to sod off, but at the same time, it's a case of grin and bear it while she figures out her escape hatch and then BOLTS breaking all manner of world sprinting records!

# What Women Want

During the Friday night flirting forays I see attempts at all kinds of approaches, and just as many aborted efforts. It's so easy it is to miss the connection because of communication break-downs, and because people won't open their mouth and say something. Anything!

Vanessa is a 33-year-old blonde who literally bubbles over with personality. She showed a LOT of promise during the early part of the night. That was before we stepped out to the bars, but then, the minute the pressure was on, her momentum just stalled. The funny thing is, she's a completely natural flirt to whom the feminine wiles come easily.

I set Vanessa couple of challenges, one involved going up to a random guy and asking for the time. She couldn't do it. She literally could not make herself turn to the bloke on her immediate left and ask what the time was. And no, she wasn't wearing a watch! The girl who'd started off as bubbly and confident at the start of the night had turned into a trembling wreck.

As I dug a little deeper, it turned out that Vanessa had been badly hurt in the past. Now she just clammed up in front of guys. It didn't matter if she fancied them or not, if a guy came within spitting distance she would just shut down. It's girls like Vanessa who actually know how to flirt, but they won't, because they're scared. Scared of meeting someone new and getting hurt all over again; so they keep their cards to their chest. No problem with that, everyone's got their own survival instinct, but I did wonder why she was out on a Flirting Mission! Hopefully it helped (although I can't say I saw much evidence of it on the night). Well like I always say, you can't win 'em all!

The point is that Vanessa needs to sort herself out and not worry too much about this flirting lark until she's *out of recovery mode*. In the meanwhile, you need to not worry about the Vanessa's and look over yonder for someone who's more appreciative! Someone like Sharna...

Sharna is 28 and cute and perky and boy, does she have an opinion on everything! That's why I was surprised that during our Girls Night Out she was happy to watch, rather than get into it. Her take on it was: *'Why on earth would you approach someone just for the sake of it?'* Fair enough. That's only the whole point of the night!

The funny thing was that she really went for it on the dance floor; but as much as she SAID she enjoyed it, she hardly smiled or chatted to anyone all night, except fro when she was dancing but then she was in her own little world which made it difficult for anyone to connect with her – not just the guys! Eventually, after much prodding and persuading, she came around to the idea that yes, we were meant to be having fun, so why not initiate a conversation with a random guy? Here's what happened. She went up to this guy who was sitting down and asked him – if her bag could have a rest on his chair – which I thought was really cute and quirky.

Unfortunately though, either the guy wasn't interested, or it was too subtle, either way, he didn't get it. So that was that. There was no chance of any further conversation. But let me put the question to you old chap – if that was you, and this super cute girl came up and asked to put her bag on the back of your chair – would you get that she wanted to chat? Or that she was making an effort to connect with you? Surely you would! I mean yes it's subtle, I get that, but for Pete's sake, if you liked the look of her, and she was being friendly, you'd talk to her right, without thinking too hard about it?

I hope so

Because when I use the expression 'drop the white hanky' that's what I'm talkin' about! Sharna dropped it but the guy didn't pick it up. End of. And for a girl like Sharna, who typically wouldn't say *boo* to anyone all night, it was a pretty brave thing to do. At least she was trying. What about you? Are you trying hard enough?

32-year-old Ann-Marie looked stunning the night she came out to Flirt Shimmy. She oozed natural charm and all the assets. The effect of her va-va voom cleavage and red glossy lips was a winner, but as she herself pointed out, she needed to learn to 'work it' – often easier said than done. Ann-Marie wanted to improve her skills, and was aware she needed a top-up. That's the reason she found herself out with me.

Things started off well with her being all warm and fuzzy and buzzing here and there. But as the night progressed, she took more of a backseat role; a temptation for so many who don't fancy being assertive when it comes to this business. After a while she just shut down completely and sat back just taking it all in. Blame it on the chemistry; blame it on the competition, blame it on the full moon – who knows what the problem was, that's not the point, there are a lot of reasons that people won't put themselves out there but what I'm interested to know is what happens when YOU encounter someone like that?

Do you could assume that they're not 'in the game' as it were? Because if you spotted Anne-Marie, or anyone like her, I can pretty much guarantee there would be no incentive to approach. Her body language is closed. She's not smiling or looking your way. And even if you do manage to get her attention, she refuses to catch your eye. She's just sat back with her arms folded watching…The problem is you fancy her, so do you risk it?

Of course it's not ideal, far from it, but for the moment, whilst Ann-Marie deals with her demons, that's the way it is. And time and time again you will come across women who look for all the world like they're not up for being approached but it's deceptive, because under the tough surface they're generally as soft as marshmallow but while their body language screams *Don't Even Think About It!* you've not got much incentive to approach! But let me ask you this, if you spot someone like Anne-Marie, and you think she's cute, could you in your wildest dreams force yourself to

116

make an approach anyway? Clearly if you did you would need the hide of an elephant, because it could go either way.

But if you did manage to build up your confidence and find the courage to venture over, there is a very good chance that she will be delighted to chat. Because in spite of her apparent lack of interest, Ann-Marie is very single and very actively wanting to date. And the truth is she doesn't really like sitting alone missing out on all the action. She's just lousy at advertising it.

This is one of those Go-Fer-It situations where taking a risk and making an approach – green light or not – might be the best thing you ever did. If not, easy come; easy go.

Clarishta was someone I'd met before, and on this hot August night she was completely up for it. And wow, did she look the part. Her glossy, toffee coloured hair shimmering atop her coffee coloured shoulders, her teeth whiter than humanely possible, she was all aglow. She had no problems when it came to making an approach either and she initiated chats with a couple of different guys right off the bat. The interesting thing was that while it seemed to start off swimmingly, there was a hiccup. The conversation kept stalling whenever she paused and left it up to the guy to keep things going. Both times he dropped the ball and refused to take the lead. What the…! So with nowhere left to go, Clarishta made her excuses and left. I don't blame her!

So here's another question for you – if someone approaches you, do you expect her to take charge of everything? Is she then expected to keep the conversation going, buy the drinks and ask for your number? Please tell me it's not so!

Whatever the reasons, Clarishta came away concluding that even when she went right up to someone with a big smile and made it easy, they still didn't come through with the goods!! Not fair guys! If we lob the ball in your direction, and you like what you see, you've got to run with it, otherwise you're not keeping your part of the bargain!

I'm telling you this because at some point you will encounter variations of all the girls we've spoken about. No doubt you have already. And while they're all sweet and adorable – they have issues. Who doesn't? We all do, and we do our best to deal with them. But for the most part, it's a case of perception versus reality. You think someone wouldn't be arsed talking to you. They think it would be great to talk to anyone, if only someone would come over and say `hi!'

It's up to you to make a judgement call and detect whether a situation is worth pursuing. Likewise, you've got to instinctively know when that ball is being lobbed in your court and you've got to smash it back. Start practicing those serves!

## New Kid On The Kop

Now that you are set to become the King of Kong-versation, you need to get up the hours of practice required. Who will you practice on and where will you go?

Describe the areas you need to work on and how you will go about that e.g. I can be awkward when it comes to starting a conversation but I'm going to try chatting with new people. Once I've done it a few times, I think I'll be fine. I'm going to try one of those approaches on a random stranger and hope for the best!

What techniques are you willing to try and what changes do you hope to see? I'll go out with different groups of people more since I find when I go out with my friends we don't talk to anybody new, ever!

What can you do immediately to open up more chatting opportunities? I'd like to give Speed-dating a go. I've never tried it and always been curious.

How will you incorporate the practice 'chat' sessions into your day-to-day? I'll spend less time with my regular drinking buddies and try to spend more time with new people I'm still getting to know.

## To summarise let's look at the Key Points

➤ Concentrate on sharpening your communication skills

➤ Practice asking a stranger something, anything!

➤ Create a Tool-Kit from which you can pull jokes and party tricks

*In a Nutshell?* Be the person who gets noticed and remembered.

## Challenges

✓ Improve your communication skills

✓ Go out of your way to have great conversation

✓ Practice the skill of listening

✓ Try the Tag Question technique at every opportunity

✓ Dish out the compliments

## KPIs: *Assess Your Progress*

➤ Made any new approaches? (Y/N)

➤ Tried any different approach techniques? (Y/N)

➤ Struck up any conversations beyond '*Hello*'? (Y/N)

➤ Practiced chatting to anyone and everyone? (Y/N)

➤ Dished out any compliments? (Y/N)

➤ Settled into the habit of using and memorising names? (Y/ )N

*Mantra:* Work your charm from the minute you leave home. Think Lights,Camera, Action!

## Checklist

✓ *Commitment*

✓ *Enthusiasm*

✓ *Confidence*

121

### *What To Do Tonight…Task #1*

Get the party started by approaching a random stranger. Go to any of the locations mentioned and find a reason to ask someone something specific, even if it's simply for directions. If you're feeling brave, road-test a few Ice-Breakers as well, and see if you have any luck opening up the conversational channels. Once you've completed the task, and you feel comfortable with making further approaches, you'll be ready to graduate to the meaty stuff. *Here's the plan:*

✓   *Approach up to three strangers, one at a time.*

✓   *Prepare ahead for what you will say and who might you encounter.*

Start with the basics, smile and ask anything relevant:

✓   *Excuse me, could you tell me where is the nearest tube/bus stop/cab rank* (fill in the blank)

You may question the point of randomly approaching a stranger with an inane query, but you will find as the week's progress and the challenges get harder that this is a necessary starting point. It goes without saying, you will need to use your imagination and above all, be ballsy. The success of these tasks depends on your input and imagination. Most importantly you have to get off the sofa and go to places where opportunities will open up.

# Q & A

*I'm OK once I get started, but I have no idea what to say when I go up to someone cold. Any suggestions...?*

Size up your environment and find the common ground. Be as observant as you can to find relevant things to talk about. Look around you and pay attention, what are the props? Where is your ammo? Refer the Ice-Breakers in the section above and come up with your own. Go out and practice when it *doesn't matter,* so you're good to go when it does. If all else fails, simply go over and introduce yourself. Women love a man with confidence. Try it. What's the worst thing that can happen?

*I've read that it's best to ask questions but then I never get to say any of the good stuff about me.*

The good news is you're halfway there. Asking questions is great, but all too often I hear feedback from women who never get to find out anything if they're the ones getting asked all the questions. The key is to find a balance. Remember the Tag Questions we talked about earlier? Where you reveal something and then open the question out, for instance: *I'm having roast lunch at my local on Sunday. What about you? What are your plans?"*

*I never know what to do when there's that horrible pause in a conversation. Where are you supposed to go from there?*

At ease Captain! The worst thing about those moments is how bad they seem to *you.* It's never really that bad. If you relax and let yourself go with it, you might find the pauses are the most useful part of a conversation. It's a chance for everyone to catch their breath. Give it a few seconds to see where it goes, and if nothing develops, feel free to change direction. Make a joke of it with a brisk, *"Moving right along!"* Ask about her plans for the day, evening, weekend, whatever. It doesn't matter what you're talking about, so long as it's her favourite subject – herself!

# Step 3. Looking and Living the Part

## Hey Good Lookin'

We're all victims of a sex obsessed world. Your appearance has a direct impact on your love life. Looking good means you stand a better chance of getting sex. (*Cheering and whooping please!*) But you already know that, so I'm not going to lecture you about every product on the market. Nor do I expect you to gad about like the God of Gucci, or morph into a sartorial joke. But since we all agree that man-ity – men's vanity – how you dress and present yourself is absolutely vital to your seduction kit, let's step it up a notch.

Let's start with your sense of style. Are you a Mr Retrosexual: a Martini drinking, dapper dude who wears bespoke suits of devastating sharpness? No? I didn't think so. Never mind! Possibly you're the broad shouldered, square jawed, grey flecked embodiment of handsomeness? Or a modern, masculine guy who dresses neatly but simply? Great! But think beyond the superficial look you're rocking. What's your vibe? Your style? And more importantly will it make those willowy, swishy haired girls fall at your feet?

Women make an extraordinary effort to look good. She's probably had two weeks of back to back beauty treatments to look that good, and it's mainly I might add, to thrill the collective YOU. So it wouldn't hurt to pay attention next time you see some hot babe whose style and attitude is heaving with more insolence than Pippa Middleton's bum. In fact every time you see a woman shimmering 'n' blinging 'n' zinging with all the bells 'n' whistles, and looking gorgeous in the process, you should respond by kicking out a few jams yourself. That's not too much to ask is it? If she looks good and she knows it – you should match that.

You already know that style isn't just about clothes. The way you put yourself together gives us the most direct visual cue about you: it's an extension of your personality, a form of self-expression, a way to reveal yourself and your way of looking at the world, without saying a thing. It's the ability to create your own look and carry off the easy swagger that comes with knowing you're well turned out. It's the way you wear an outfit and how you carry yourself that makes you look confident. The ability to wear something that makes you stand tall with your shoulders back and feel '*yeah!*' *Yet*, they say the most intelligent men attach the least importance to the way they dress – please say it's not true! You need to make an effort for women. Why?

Generally speaking male vanity is appreciated by fashion loving females; even though we don't necessarily understand men's fashion, on account of the fact that you only seem to wear a variation of shirts and jeans! We do have certain expectations when it comes to how you look. And when we meet you for the first time, we will size you up, and form an instant impression based on your overall sense of style and image. From that we will be able to deduce that, '*Aha/ You've actually put some effort into this!*' It shows you've got healthy self-esteem! Tick box please! So whatever you think – we are paying attention. If we like what we see, we might even smile at you across the room.

The big question is – how motivated are you to bother about looking your best? And how hard are you working the connection between looking good and meeting women? Because if you're not, your outfit selection will put you at a severe disadvantage in the pulling field. The thing is, as long as you're serious about this crazy little notion of looking good and attracting women effortlessly, there are a trillion ways to go about it, but it does takes time and planning. You really need to commit to being consistently appealing with an upbeat self-image. That means you might need to rethink your current look.

Women have a trillion weird and wonderful quirks when it comes to what they like and what they don't. It goes without saying that the way you look and present yourself is appealing to a particular type of woman. Generally though, women are attracted to guys whose sense of style reveals

127

something about them – the appeal of a chap with individuality is not to be underestimated. Some girls like their preppy boys, while others like their men to be all dirty rock n roll: grizzled, tattooed and hairy. Others go for skinny jeans and floppy fringes, while some want for nothing more than a buff butt in fitted Levis and quality T-Shirt over hairless chest. Or we might be turned off by your wholesome top-to-toe peppiness and want to get in there and rip your t-shirt right up while we muss your hair and scuff up your sneakers!

If on the other hand you're rocking a bohemian indie look that's frankly bordering on minging, and you're mistaken for a homeless fella whilst waiting for the tube, then, you might want to clean up your act up a little. By all means go ahead and unleash your inner rockstar, but know that few women will appreciate you looking like you've just emerged from three days of feral sex in a tent.

Likewise if you're trying to be someone you're NOT with your style choices that will be evident as well. Maybe you're kitted out in preppy loafers purely because you heard they're bang on trend, or rocking a ruffled devil-may-care attitude topped off with a: *"The More I Drink, The Better You Look"* T-Shirt? If so, you might want to rethink that. Your sense of style and the clothes you wear should represent the person you are – that way there's less chance of confusion later.

Whilst some women are only looking at your logos and labels, just the shallow ones, most are more interested in the kind of person you are. Certainly if you reveal your wealth and status with loads of designer bling tumbling off you, then of course you will attract a certain kind of woman. Likewise if you wear your most rumpled McScruffy clobber everywhere, you should know what to expect. It's a matter of personal taste. You can't possibly know what tickles her fancy. The best you can do is stick to the style that feels right for you. By the same token, if you find yourself fancying a woman who doesn't respond well to your image, or suggests endless ways to make you change, you might be best to accept that she's not 'getting' you. If she's not getting you, you have to ask yourself if you're in the right situation. Take that one step further and, if you find a woman who is desperate to change you, or more insidiously, 'mould' you, you should be hearing alarm bells.

Her doggedness to change you is likely to be part of a much bigger issue about power games and control issues. If you buckle and go along with it, it could develop into all sorts of simmering resentment down the track. If she doesn't approve of your look and you comply with her wishes, you're setting a precedent for the future – where she can walk all over you. At which point I've got just one thing to say – if you're happy with the look you're rocking, then Men, stand your ground! Having said that, if all you ever get is negativity about your sense of style, you might want to rethink it.


*Livvy is one fearless and bold woman, I'm not sure of her age but I'd say late 30s – and sassy is the word. She is a looker and oh boy, does she have the confidence to work it. Her style is a full on sexy diva vibe. She's all skimpy skirts, long legs, killer heels and tiny tops. If you saw Livvy in action you would either go in for the kill, or run in the other direction. That's because the Livvies of the world aren't for everyone. It's a brave man (or a very drunk man) who makes an approach. And perhaps not surprisingly, Livvy attracts the players which as it turns out, suits her quite well. You see she's one of those women who is very clear about the kind of guy she will and won't talk to. Her specifications are very narrow. He needs to be kitted out in gold chains and designer garb for starters. We are talking major bling. Anything less than that falls under her radar. The thing about Livvy is that thinks she's England's answer to Beyoncé. Advance her by all means, and so long as you're rocking a look that's as bold as hers, you'll be fine. If not, good luck!*

## Style Guru

When it comes to revamping your image, a woman's opinion is crucial. So no matter how sharp you think your style, no doubt you could do with some insider's advice. I'm talking straight from the horse's mouth. That's where your Style Guru comes into it, someone who will advise on grooming and fashion choices. If there isn't a friendly female at hand, consider asking a work pal or a family member whose taste you trust. Since you're looking for someone in your demographic, you might want to move on from your mum, unless she is a proper professional style guru of course.

Ask your lady friend her opinion on everything, from aftershave to shoes, suits and shirts. Chances are you think you look OK once you're all suited and booted but the reality is, you can probably look a hell of a lot better. Women are sticklers for detail. Your image reveals more about your personal habits, than you might like to think. Lose your shyness and invite a platonic lady friend to accompany you on a shopping trip. Do your research first and take along magazine cut-outs, or pictures of the looks you like. It could save you a lot of money on 'impulse buys' – those items you buy and never, ever wear.

Study old photos and pick out your favourite looks. What do you like best about the way you looked at that time? What about the way you look now? Be honest! Once you accept the way you are now, and your potential, you'll be better positioned to restyle yourself. Likewise, until you are clear about your best assets, you won't be able to showcase them. Nor will you succeed in improving your weaknesses until you've identified them – only then can you proceed in a productive way.

If you don't have a style guru sorted out, then one alternative – only for the very brave – is to hit the stores and once you've selected something to try on, collar a woman passer-by for her opinion. And before you gasp and say: *'I couldn't possibly!'* Hear me out because personally speaking, I get this a lot, at least once every couple of weeks, and I never think anything of it. I've been asked for advice on suits, shirts, belts, ties – you name it. I'm always happy to help out with the female point of view. In fact I'm delighted.

Initially you need to look to the area that needs the most work and embark upon a quick self-critique. How is your wardrobe doing? Is it a DUD: Dated? Uninspired? Dreary? All a bit of the Emperor with No Clothes syndrome? Are you well overdue for some well fitted trousers and cheerful shirts in flattering colours? There's a lot to be gained by trying new looks and revamping yourself through wardrobe adjustments. Eventually you'll get to the point where, through trial and error, you will look and feel cool. Think about the colours and styles that will liven up your wardrobe and make you feel like the Mati-freakin-Hara. It's fine to mix up styles and colours – so long as you know what you're doing. Plan a trip to your local H & M store, or get online at a dependable menswear website, like, www.mrporter.com, and acquire some new attire ASAP!

Once you've thought about how you would like to look, ask yourself how close that is to the look you're currently rocking? And is that look working for you? Or do you look like you're trying too hard when you go out to chat up girls? Perhaps you shuffle uncomfortably in a get up that looks eye-wateringly cool, but makes you feel awkward and self-conscious? Or you might be guilty of committing illegal fashion crimes? If so, how would you know that? Fashion choices are personal. You should wear whatever you want. Just wear it with flair.

### *Be realistic, there are rules about how to dress:*

- ➤  Low slung jeans with five inches of pants showing are fine – if you're under 18

- ➤  Skin-tight vests are fine – if you've got the body of an Olympian athlete

- ➤  Sandals with socks are fine – if you're a Norwegian farmer

- ➤  Collared shirts with round neck jumpers are fine – if you're a Vicar

- Army fatigues are fine – if you're hiking in rural England

- Tummy ticklers or tank-tops are fine – if you're a 14 year old girl

- Cravats, tartan trousers and bow-ties are fine – if you can pull it off

- Bare chests are fine for the beach or the pool – and that's all

   *Get my drift?*

### What About Accessories, Eh?

Wearing quirky accessories is useful for a couple of reasons, firstly it gives us a peek inside your personality; secondly it gives us something that we can comment on, women do it all the time and it makes it easier for you! So it makes sense that by wearing accessories, you give us something to compliment; otherwise it's difficult when all we've got to work with is, *"Nice shirt, nice shoes, nice shirt, nice...erm"*

It's not just what you wear either, it's what you carry as well, and it works both ways. By accessorising well you're drawing attention to yourself and making it easier for someone to notice you. Likewise when you spot someone you fancy and they're accessorising madly, they're literally giving you a reason to saunter over and say *'Wow, I love your..."*

So rather than spluttering, *"But, but, but... I'm a bloke! I wouldn't be seen dead in accessories"* hear me out. I'm not suggesting you wear strands of string bangles and Puka shells, I'm talking about proper fashion forward accessories as ice-breakers and conversational props.

Take as your inspiration the James Bond themed fashion shows. Thanks to the age of technology and gadgets which have taken centre stage, we have more opportunities than ever to reveal something quirky about our personality. Attention-grabbing accessories and interesting bits and bobs can be worn as well as carried, from iPods and crazily coloured earphones, to shoes that shout Attitude, statement ties and slogan T-Shirts, snug fitting jeans, fingerless gloves, hats, and skilfully tailored dinner jackets – they all work as ice-breakers.

*My good friend Lynette met her guy at the Isle of Wight music festival. He was wearing a Kings of Leon T-Shirt. She loves Kings of Leon. Bingo! Another smartly shod friend became infatuated with a guy she kept running into on the train platform. She was smitten by his vast array of quirky ties. Finally she found it within herself to go up and compliment him. As it turns out he'd been admiring her as well. Yess!*

*Anoushka, another good friend in her early 30s has announced that she will only date guys who wear watches. What the?? Ask her why and she'll tell you that she can't see herself being with a guy who depends on his mobile phone to find out the time. She just prefers someone who makes the effort to wear a watch. Fair enough! Another friend Lisa says she will only date guys who wear preppy loafers and polo shirts – even on the weekend. I told her that David Cameron is spoken for!*

Thanks to my job I spend a lot of time trawling London's cafes and bars which puts me in the perfect position to experiment with what works and what doesn't. And I can tell you right now, accessorising works, big time, regardless of whether you're male or female. I get comments all the time. I make it easy for guys by accessorising. They find ways to get my attention by noticing the props whether it's my pink mini-laptop and matching phone, a blinging pair of shoes, a book, an interesting looking bag or a travel guide – it doesn't matter what it is. What matters is that you carry something around that's worth commenting on. Anything that says, *"I'm interesting. Really!"*

And be on the lookout for women who are wearing, or carrying props. I can't tell you the number of times I've been sitting, tapping away at my keyboard and men's curiosity gets the better of them – they use that as part of their approach. I provide the props, they comment on them. It's a team effort! So when you notice a woman wearing something amazing, or carrying something that you can comment on – recognise that moment and jump on it. Hopefully, she'll do the same!

And it's not just what you wear, it's also what you drink. According to Christina Hendricks from *Mad Men*: "*We want you to order Scotch. "It's the most impressive drink order. It's classic. It's sexy. Such a rich colour. The glass, the smell. It's not watered down with fruit juice. It's Scotch. And you ordered it."*

### *Do you tick her shoebox?*

So you know that women judge a man on his shoes, right? "*Yes, yes."* You groan. *"We learnt that when we were five."* Good! Because If you want sex – you need to wear good shoes. It really is that simple. Hands down, this is the most important accessory you can have. Don't be shy about investing big-time here because you will dazzle us blind if you get this right. This is where the best statements are made – a fact the fashion industry have cottoned onto. There's your everyday shoe, and your dress shoe, but whether you put on your blue suede shoes, loafers, Docs or wing-tip brogues, dress to impress – shoes must be quality and they must be shiny. My good friend Joe has the most incredible shoe collection, and no matter where he is, or what he's doing, he's always rocking a pair of the super shiniest red or electric blue pointy-toes and he gets complimented on them everywhere he goes. He's practically famous for them! That will make anyone feel good. *C'mon Twinkle toes!*

### *Sock horror!*

➢ Invest in 10 pairs of matching socks

➢ Buy just one pair of look-at-me-shoes

➢ Prepare in advance so you're never caught unawares

➢ Splash out on a suit that makes you look and feel better than ever

➢ Update your pants drawer!

### It's all Pants!

Are you a style scrooge? Do you live in blissful oblivion of Armani and scrimp on your pants and get around in saggy greying Y-fronts? If so you need to update as a matter of urgency! And you need to think laterally. You will find a treasure chest of fun in the Men's Underwear department of any store. From men's girdles to Bum Holders: pants with engineering to keep your bum nice and perky to Booster Pants that come with their own inbuilt 'package', I kid you not! You can buy a bigger package if you're not happy with what nature bestowed on you. Of course I'm not entirely sure what happens if you get lucky, and your playmate discovers that, *'Oops!'* that 'package' was a little misleading. You could argue that it's no different to the wonder bras that women have been wearing since the year dot, and you would be right. But I don't know; somehow, that seems a little less weird! And there'll be no Budgie Smugglers thanks, in fact when it comes to trunks, think about it before you go and flash your best bits. Just because Daniel Craig can get away with it, doesn't mean you can!

X-Factor Judge and hottie Kelly Rowland is a big fan of the English lad and has quite the thing for British lads' erm, behinds. *"Have you seen how cute they wear their pants [trousers]?"* She said to Cosmopolitan. *"All neat and tight"* Apparently she also has a soft spot for fellow judge, Gary Barlow's hiney (her word). At this rate, it could be yours next!

### Five Things To Know About Men's Stuff...

➢ Booster Pants come with their own inbuilt 'package'

➢ You can buy Men's girdles, or 'Guy-dles' in any dept store

➢ Bum Holders are pants with engineering to keep your bum perky

➢ Guy-liner is eye-liner made for men

➢ Man-scara is mascara made for men

➢ Man-kini –Never to be worn by any one other than Sacha Baron Cohen!

➢ VPL is your Visible Penis Line

135

### Get Your Strawberries Out There Lad!

Doing something racy and risqué to transform your appearance can lead to all sorts of adventures, so why not transform yourself with a look that you've always aspired to, but never been brave enough to try? Whether that's a new hairstyle, a piercing, or a tattoo. If you do crave a tattoo, be sure to think it through first, since tattoos aren't just for Christmas. Likewise any permanent or semi-permanent changes you make to your body will encourage others to form the basis of their opinion about you. Tattoos and piercings are a very personal taste, whether you want to pierce your tongue or your privates – it's a niche look. As a result, you will limit your appeal in the marketplace. Simply put, some girls will find it absolutely the most yuck thing in the world. Others will find it the biggest turn on. And since you never know where you're going to put your winky, you might want to think about before doing anything rash!

### Tattoos

✓   *Choose your design and take a photo into the consultation – before making an appointment to get anything done.*

✓   *Visit up to two or three different places for a consultation to suss out the practitioner as you're likely to end up spending hours and hours with them, so it's important you meet them first, and see if you like them.*

✓   *Give yourself a 'cooling off' period before you pay your deposit*

✓   *Don't do it while you're drunk or otherwise enhanced!*

### Props & Icebreakers to kick some flirting ass

✓   *Hat/Scarf/Statement belt*

✓   *Pocket Watch/Key Chain Distinctive Cuffs/Tie Pin*

✓   *Cigarette holder/lighter*

### Spex in the City

Johnny Depp knows how to rock a pair of glasses, and there's absolutely no reason you can't. If you're sporting unflattering eye-wear, don't! Ditch the glasses that cramp your style and take your Style Guru along on a mission to select a new pair. Specsavers offer an in-store computerised camera service for this exact purpose. I don't know anyone who hasn't dramatically improved their look once they started wearing a frame that actually suited them. Sort yourself out in the eyewear department if you want discerning women to drape themselves all over you because, newsflash – we love a man in glasses. We think it makes you look highbrow. And that's hot. Kerching!   While we're on the subject, a pair of cool sunglasses can look hot, and also give you the psychological advantage if you don't want to give away what you're thinking!

### Best and Worst Looks Seen Across London

✓  *Crisp tailored charcoal grey suit and pale blue shirt*

✓  *Matching tan belt and shoes*

✓  *Fitted black silk shirt*

✓  *Mauve dress shirt with black trousers*

✓  *Red sneakers*

✓  *Blue velvet Docs*

✓  *Red Jeans*

✓  *Rocky T-Shirt (on a seriously buff guy)*

### Worst

✗   *iPood T-Shirt (What the...?)*

✗   *Mr Perfect T-Shirt*

✗   *Pastel pink too tight T-Shirt*

✗   *Pornstar T-Shirt*

✗   *Lime green psychedelic shirt and matching shorts*

✗   *Black leather short shorts*

✗   *White shorts, shirts and sneakers with black socks!*

### Branded T-Shirts:

*Slogan T-Shirt's can be a good ice-breaker, so long as you choose them wisely.*

✓   *Wearing "I ♥ Children with Leukaemia" on your T-shirt might convince us you're a nice guy, in the same way that....*

*"Let's Get Nekkid and Shag!" T-shirt will not!*

**Judges Verdict:** *Dress age appropriately and brainstorm with your style guru. If you wear something that gets loads of compliments, buy one in every colour!*

➤   *Top Tip*: Don't take style tips from British politicians!

## If You Look Good, You Can Get Away With Anything...

Nothing says, *'No sex thanks!'* like a cold sore on your person; so let's get right down to the tic-tacs – how is your grooming regime? Are you fresh and fragrant? Crisp and laundered? Groomed and manicured? Or are your hands are so hairy that you need to comb them? If so, may I suggest you address that? While you're there, might I enquire about your excess facial fuzz – how's it looking? Or is it keeping the babes away? What about your post-acne skin – is it letting you down? Whatever it is, make a pact to improve it. Once you put in the time to step up the grooming, you'll notice the progress immediately.

It's pretty safe to say that most women don't find the whiff of unwashed hair, or a grimy neck particularly alluring. I spend many a long day at public libraries and I'm always shocked by the fetid smells on some of the men, both older and younger, as they come and go. The thing is I honestly don't think they're aware of it. They might be clean, but the stench is in their clothes. That's what happens when you don't do the laundry regularly or wear a deodorant. And pity the woman who goes in for a cheeky kiss on the cheek because she will cop it from where it's worst – the upper chest, under-arm area – and I can tell you – it's a massive turn off.

Gone are the days when the man who looked after himself was considered gay, today it's MAN-datory – take a bow David Beckham! We want you to look good, smell good, and taste good. We want you to wash your hands after the toilet, and *before* you touch us. We want shiny shoes, matching socks and gunk-free nails. We want to look at you and automatically start humming the Kings of Leon tune: *"Your sex is on fire!"*

If you haven't ventured into one of the many unisex stores on the High Street offering men's treatments from facials to waxing – why not give it a whirl? Whether it's for a cleansing facial, or you're ridding yourself of the dreaded nasal hair, get onto it pronto. The same with taming your beloved mono-brow – just bin it! If you're sporting a massive HOB, or hair-of-the-back, and you don't want to risk making the girls cry – wax it the hell-o off! And don't even think about a DIY job, because half a tube of shaving foam and a blunt razor later, your back will be a bloodied mess – then we really will run crying into the street!

Re-organise your toiletries and grooming kit so that any stale products are chucked, replenished and replaced every few months (rubbing stale shaving cream onto your face is like rubbing grime into it). Then prepare to restock. All the brand names do comprehensive skin care ranges for men, but it can be confusing unless you know what you're doing.

Keep it simple. Start with some online research to find which brand is best for you, then it's a trip to Boots or your local department store. Be warned, once the sales assistant has you in her clutches, it will be hard to leave without having bought half the store!

So, while it would be boring to go on and on about men's style (that's what GQ Magazine is for) there's no excuse not to present a polished version of yourself every time you step out the door; whether you're a nice-armed chap, a well-of-the-behind chap, or simply a well turned out chap – no excuses. Too bad if you weren't dealt the hand with the 'Most Handsome Man on the Planet' card!

Indeed if that is the case, you need to work smarter to make the most of what you've got. Likewise if you don't have R-Patz face to present to the world, don't despair, you can still do a heck of a lot to improve things. Apply the motto to work with what you've got! You only have to look at early footage of the Right Hon Simon Cowell, pre-TV fame, to see what I mean.

The guy's clearly had more work on his face than the Home Improvement Show. We're talking the whole shebang: dental surgery, teeth veneers, Botox, tinted lashes, waxing of the chest, designer suits, fake tan, lashings of man-scara (mascara) – but hey, it's working for him. Rewind a few years back and you'll see that he had one of the plainest mugs on TV. Now he looks more like Clooney's younger brother every day – albeit less gorgeous. It's called upkeep and it's expensive which is fine for Cowell since he's a Superpower, and he's working it. But unless your career depends on making a living from TV, there's really no need to go that far.

It's never too late to start a skin-care routine, one which you will to stick to in the long-term. It only takes a minute to slap on some gunk, so make a pact to cleanse and moisturise skin daily – and tone too if you're really keen. Keep your lips moist with lashings of super strength lip-balm and hydrate by drinking loads of water. Remember also to protect your skin from the harsh climate by using SPF in the summer and heavier product in the winter. Do this every day and try not to drink all the beer in Britain and you will stand a better chance of looking good for the next fifty years.

Want to feel fragrant? Well go right ahead, but be smart about it, otherwise there are some cheap and nasty fragrances out there that will send us running. And while something basic like the utilitarian CK might work its magic, why not try something a little more distinctive that the ladies won't recognise at one hundred paces? Keep in mind that while most us of enjoy a splash of sexy-time aftershave – and will swoon if you smell fabulous even if you look a bit mingin'– we don't want you drowning in it. Think passion not petrol fumes. It's the same with deodorant, by all means use it, but refrain from liberal use of those highly perfumed toxic deodorants that stink loudly over our perfume into sweaty armpits. The danger of overdoing it, apart from the obvious, is that it could clash violently with the scent we're wearing.

What about your smile? Do women gaze dreamily at your pearly white dazzlers? I suspect not! Not unless you've had a lot of cosmetic dentistry – which if we're honest, is not the norm for the average Briton. But never mind, even if you did inherit wobbly teeth from the wonky side of the family, Dr. Smile is here to save the day. You can make massive improvements thanks to the wonders of modern dentistry. And while a complete overhaul will set you back a pretty penny, investing in a simple whitening procedure or a basic clean is not only affordable, it will result in a noticeable and instantaneous improvement as well as correcting yellowing or stained teeth. You want a killer smile. Go get it tiger!

*Hair*: If you've been rocking the same look for the past decade and you're feeling ripe for a change, best to skip the barber and see a stylist. Find out what suits you and stick with it. Whether you're a Mr Wash & Go, or your hair is glistening in a sea of product, use a decent conditioner. If you've got dandruff, annihilate it! If you're a silver fox, wear it with style. If you're follicly challenged deal with it. If you're a baldy, wear it with pride – and forget about trying to hide impending baldness under a hat, it will only make us more anxious about what's under there – or not under there! Keep in mind there's nothing unsexier than a guy who's more into his hair than we are!

*Brows*: A good brow tidy is easy to come by and it's important, especially if we're talking mono-brow monster! Get yourself along to any department store and get cleaned up with a quick and efficient threading process, or a good old-school waxing. Either way, you'll be done in a matter of minutes. Word of warning – don't go overboard and don't let your brows get too tidy or you'll start looking like a Gok Wan wannabe.

*Nails*: It's very important that you pay attention to your nails because everybody else will! The need to be trimmed, tidy and clean. If you can't manage the maintenance yourself, get them done professionally. And sort your toe-nails out while you're there, nothing worse than getting scratched by a long toe nail right at the worst possible moment. Yikes!

*Make-up*: erm sorry, look more men wear make-up than you realise, and not just for fancy dress or KISS inspired glam rock, it's used to hide blemishes and improve one's over-all look. Don't knock it till you've tried it. The trick is to know what you're doing and wear it with subtlety. Take your pick of tinted moisturisers, eye-liner; man-scara, or bronzer. Then find a nice lady friend to help with the application.

*Fake tan*: Don't try this at home unless you want to become an Oompa Loompa. For best results, book in for a professional application.

*Ears*: Wax growing out of your ears? Well c'mon, get rid of it; you're not a Neanderthal!

*Nasal Hair*: Book extra time at the Barbers if you've got the dreaded nasal hair explosion.

In order be a babe magnet you need to look good but, don't spend so long in the bathroom that you end up taking longer than us to get ready. As much as we want you germ free, it has been scientifically proven that women are not attracted to men who are more coiffed than us. We can't have you putting us to shame! So if you come out of this looking like a perfumed chimp – take a bow Ronaldo – we will find that extremely off putting. We like the idea that our men are too busy indulging in you know, manly things, to spend too long pampering and preening. As modern as we are, we still want you to be a proper man!

### *Just The Tonic*

✓ *Step up your image*

✓ *Recruit a style guru*

✓ *Rescue dry/damaged hair with a deep conditioning treatment*

✓ *Have a facial, complete with steam, exfoliation and extraction*

✓ *Do a close up in a naturally lit mirror before leaving the house*

✓ *Practice excellent hygiene at all times so you don't get caught unprepared!*

- ➢ BLOKE QUOTE: In 2011 newly reinvented metrosexual Shane Warne admitted to using moisturiser and losing weight. *"Being healthy is now a daily habit. I feel great."* He didn't mention the other little helpers.

- ➢ Simon Cowell says having Botox is like, *"Cleaning his teeth."* Technically they're not his teeth though are they?

- ➢ Piers Wotsit who used to work with Simon says, *"Botox is part of the job"*. So is sucking Simon erm....

- ➢ Wayne Rooney *"My game's perfect, so my hair should be too"*.

- ➢ Ewan McGregor: *"I have to ask my wife, do I look like a cock or is this alright, the way I'm dressed. Because you don't want to be 'that' guy."* Observer Magazine 2/10/2011

### *Watchdog Lookouts!*

- ✗ *Don't sit in a public place and pick your nose*

- ✗ *Don't sit in a public place and scratch your bollocks!*

- ✗ *Don't sit in a public place without your shirt!*

- ✗ *Don't sit in a public place and pick the wax from your ears before studying it!*

- ✓ *Do a rear-view mirror check to make sure nothing dodgy is going on from the rear!*

- ✓ *Carry antibacterial gel in your man-bag everywhere you go.*

- ✓ *Lose the sex repellents. That includes any live growths festering out of your ears!*

# Let's Get Physical

But life's not just about dressing smartly and good grooming, one must exercise as well, otherwise your ego could be writing cheques your body can't cash. The way your body looks says a whole lot about your lifestyle so, you need to be on top of it. If you're waddling around like a floppy, puffy lump, then it's a pretty good indication that you're, erm, a floppy, puffy lump. Likewise, if you're ripped with bulging builder's biceps and a perfectly honed and toned six-pack, we're likely to assume you're gay. Holy buns of steel Batman, you just can't win!

Or maybe you can because if there's one thing you cannot do, it is speculate about women's taste. In the same way that women can't assume what you like and don't like. Thankfully most women prefer something completely different to the conventional norm. For the most part our preferences are wholly unexpected. The most unlikely girl in the world could find your wicked combination of bespectacled geekiness brilliantly, erotically sexy, proof that not all women are obsessed with the physical side of things. For a girl who doesn't do blonde chaps, I found myself developing rather a crush on Mentalist star, Simon Baker. Grrr. Yet, Robert Pattinson, who's repeatedly been named sexiest Man of the Year, does nothing for me. *'Why so pale!'* It's a very personal thing, and subjective. As the *Sex and the City* girls' say: *"Good on paper. Bad in bed!"*

At the end of the day we all have our highly individual tastes – thankfully! Imagine how boring it would be if we all had the same taste. So even if you approach someone you don't rate as an obvious match, and you suspect that together the pair of you look like the odd-squad, who cares? Give it a whirl anyway. You never know. Besides, what do you have to lose?

At the end of the day it's not all about biceps and buffness is it? Pretty much without exception, every woman I've ever asked, *'What are you looking for in a man?'* has responded in the same way:

145

> *"We want someone who makes us laugh."*

> *"We want someone we like being around."*

> *"We want someone who likes us."*

So don't fall into the trap of writing us off because: *"Oh, she'd only go for the tall, dark chiselled type."* That is such a cliché and so often not the case.

While we're on the subject, let's talk about HER looks. How important are they to you? Does she have to be a 10 plus for you to even look twice at her? If so, is that realistic? Or are you punching WAY above your weight?

There is no doubt a style or a particular look that is physically attractive to you, whether that's conventional good looks or something more quirky. How hung up are you on the whole notion of conventional looks? Personally, I find it boring. I've got my own quirky taste and it's quite unlike anyone else's – and I pride myself on that. Since I'm not exactly the conventional size zero Barbie-esque Blonde myself it works just fine. Hopefully you have your own individual taste as well.

Is there any such thing as going after someone who's supposedly out of your league? I have mixed feelings on this. One on hand I believe that if you're confident enough – you can have whoever you want. On the other hand, it pays to be realistic. And that means setting your sights on your aesthetic equal.

In order to do that you need some insight as to whether or not you're both on the same step when it comes to looks. Give yourself a honest to goodness mark out of ten for your physical appearance, if you can't do it then ask a mate – not someone who's going to treat the whole thing as a big laugh, someone who gets where you're coming from. Use the same criteria when you meet girls.

I'm always surprised by the number of hot girls I see with the plainest looking guys, though they do say that girl's are more into personality than looks – agree or disagree?

It's also said that men are more influenced by looks than girls – which means you've effectively reduced the number of potential partners you can on the basis that they don't live up to your expectation of what Mrs Wonderful should *look like*.

When was the last time you talked, really talked with someone who didn't meet your ideal of physical perfection, but found you had an amazing connection with? And if that happened did you chose not to see her again because of the way she looked, or rather didn't look? Not because she wasn't attractive, far from it, but because she wasn't what you had in mind? If that has been your experience, you might want to broaden your horizons. It's not worth limiting yourself to this ridiculous stereotype. Take a chance on someone who is smart and funny and sassy even if she's not your idea of physical perfection, you might be surprised what can happen when you start to fall in love with the essence of someone. Their beauty can literally bloom right in front of your eyes. One day you could wake up and realise that you are going out with the most beautiful girl in the word – spiritually, physically, emotionally – and you very nearly passed her over because she wasn't an identikit to what you had in mind. Get over it dude! Relax your guidelines. Try something different. Don't be such a twat and see what you find.

Think of how many unassuming men you see with drop dead stunning women. I see them everyday! Women love the strangest things for which there is no logic. Some like their quirky boffins, preppy boys, pretty boys, shy boys or stocky, bald guys. Others like their sports loving cricket-mad-cavemen – take a bow Liz Hurley. While other girls love their short

147

guys: why look over there, it's supermodel Sophie Dahl towering gleefully over teeny-jazz-whizz, Jamie Cullen.

At the end of the day it doesn't matter whether you look like David Beckham or Fester from the Adam's Family, well OK maybe it does, but the point is that whatever look you are rocking – you will absolutely do it for someone out there. No matter whether you're short, tall, stocky, fat or skinny – you are going to rock someone's world. You just won't know whose – until you give it a go.

Likewise, women favour very different body parts. For some it's a chunky set of man-hands that do it. For others it's bums. For many more, it's the thighs – massive thighs that could squeeze the living daylights out of them. For the rest of us it's the trim tums, narrow hips, bulging biceps and broad shoulders, with a special mention for the forearms. A solid pair of forearms in action can be a real turn on, especially when those forearms are carrying out the world's most important task, like erm, lifting a beer bottle. Why? Who knows? Maybe it's got something to do with the prehistoric notion of men going out into the wilds to forage. Whatever the reason, it works. So, regardless of what you like and don't like, don't be assuming there are parts of you that we won't like, we might just surprise you!

### *Top 5 Fave Body Parts*

✓   *Bums*

✓   *Chunky set of man-hands*

✓   *Biceps and shoulders*

✓   *Massive thighs that could squeeze the living daylights out of her*

✓   *Special mention for the forearms*

The minute you start getting physical you'll feel more in tune with your body. Perfection is not the goal when it comes to body types; it's simply about having the body you are comfortable with, and being happy in your own skin. But if groups of children on the street are pointing and laughing at your overgrown man-boobs, and your beer-belly is making you self-conscious and sluggish – then clearly you need to work on it.

Alternatively, if you are well into your fitness, and thanks to obsessive work outs with your personal trainer, formerly an SAS dude, your body is ripped like the proverbial, then that is the crème fraiche on the scones. But if you find that every available waking hour is spent in the gym and consequently your complexion is starting to resemble the crème fraiche on the scones – then you need to get out of the gym and into the real world. By all means be the buffest you can be, just don't spend all your time in the exercise room. B-o-r-i-n-g!

Start by varying your exercise routine and source fun new ways to get fit and fight flab. Variety is the spice of life so get out into the fresh air and energise yourself. Throw yourself around in a wrestling match, or get out in the park and hoon around on a skateboard. Get together with mates for some serious physical exertion and work-out at places where you'll have a chance of actually, you know, connecting with new people. Try something crazy and cool and fun, like motor cross sports, surfing or skiing. Take up rollerblading, rowing or rockabilly dancing. Join one of the many organised hiking tours around the UK, or simply walk everywhere.

### *You Look Good on the Dance floor!*

A man who can handle himself on the dance-floor is incredibly sexy, but if you do it really badly – I'm talking sticking your bum out and doing the Chicken-Dance – then, you need an honest appraisal from femme friends. If you do get taken gently aside and told that, in spite of what you think, that dude, you are one hell of a dodgy dancer; then you need to sort it out. There are plenty of classes where you can do just that, so do that. Be gone ye jazz hands!

Once you hit the dance-floor to throw out a few shapes, don't forget to smile. Otherwise what can happen is that you're so hell-bent on looking good with those sprayed on jeans and killer moves that you forget about connecting. Be smooth on the dance-floor by all means, but keep it light and fun, remember to maintain eye-contact, and look happy! Don't for the love of god sing-along or serenade her on a crowded dance-floor because you're not Tom Cruise and she's not Kelly McGillis. It doesn't matter what the song is, you'll only embarrass the living daylights out of her; unless she specifically encourages it of course, and then you can go hell for leather.

Whatever you end up doing, it doesn't matter whether you sink or swim because there is a life jacket. You're chasing thrills to get your blood pumping whilst reminding yourself that you're alive! Concentrate on the bonuses: a healthy complexion, revamped social life and most importantly, access to the action women who thrive on looking after their bodies with high energy hobbies! The reality is that if you're even a tiny bit toned, us women will be delighted.

### *Top 3 Things You Like Most About Your Appearance?*

✓ Height

✓ Slim-build

✓ Broad shoulders

### *Exercise Your Way to Celeb Physique*

Racing legend Lewis Hamilton swears by extensive hiking part of his vigilant exercise routine. Likewise Johnny Deep says walking is great for your butt. What better recommendation can you get? Seriously!

✓ *Do one healthy thing every day*

✓ *Get a massage and revel in that touchy-feely-feel-good therapy*

✓ *Increase your energy levels by eating fresh food*

✓ *Make exercise choices based on opportunities to meet people*

✓ *Use Schwarzenegger posture to show off your physique – whatever your size*

✓ *Throw that chest out and walk tall*

✓ *Don't slump. It's not flattering and will add years!*

✓ *Walk everywhere!*

# I Need a Hero!

If you want to be the best you can, you need to look to the Pros. Let's rewind back in time and look at the characteristics of the great Casanovas throughout history. Interestingly the men who were renowned for their seduction prowess weren't exactly eye-candy. Rather, it was their charisma and the special power they held over women – it was their ability to make them feel special that made them so memorable.

Former Prime Minister and notorious seducer, Benjamin Disraeli had the uncanny ability to make a woman feel extraordinarily special. As one woman who had dinner with Disraeli and another political heavyweight commented: *"When I left the dining room after sitting next to Mr Gladstone, I thought he was the cleverest man in England. But, after sitting next to Mr Disraeli, I thought I was the cleverest women in England."*

I rest my case!

Jean Paul Sartre the great philosopher took a different approach to seduction. Far from being eye-candy, he was not the prettiest picture in the book by any stretch of the imagination, but still, the women swarmed around him. What was his secret? According to his autobiography he became painfully aware as a teenager that he didn't have the looks to seduce women, so he devised a cunning plan to develop his intellect and his confidence to snare them. And lo and behold, throughout his life he courted many exotic and beautiful women. So yes, you could say it worked.

According to the memoirs of Casanova, at times a soldier, spy and adventurer, but most famously known as the Erotic Hero of the 18th Century – the trick was to evoke warmth, gratitude and perhaps most importantly, trust within a woman. According to those who studied the secrets to his seduction, Casanova strove to be the ideal escort in the first act: witty, charming, confidential and helpful in the second act, before moving into the bedroom in the third act. Nice work if you can get it.

### 30 Second Quiz: Spot the Biggest Flirt

There's no right or wrong in this game, it's simply a matter of coming up with your own opinion. The choice of who's hot and who's not is a personal one, so you're welcome to make-up your own list and narrow it down to those whose personality, style or image is complimentary to your own. Have a squiz at the examples provided here to get some food for thought. The idea is to pinpoint the traits within others that you find appealing, and hopefully along the way, find characteristics you identify with.

### Toast Your Glasses To...Your Heroes

Who are your heroes? Who do you admire? Can you name any rock stars, politicians or sportsmen that inspire you? Put on your fantasy hat for a minute and suppose that someone came along and said, *"Take this pill and you can be whoever you want to be"*. Who would you choose to be?

Now think about what makes you respond to those you admire. It's all very well to say that they're cool, in the same way I would drool and say that Johnny Depp and Dave Grohl and sex-on-legs Jon Hamm from *Mad Men* are cool – but let's get down to tic-tacs. What is it exactly?

Is it their style and image? Their mannerisms and character? Or the way they rock a particular look? Maybe it is quite simply their charisma. Whatever it is, break it down to individual features. Identify what you like about them and why. Try to be specific. What characteristics do they have that you recognize? Are there any you can adapt? That's not to say you're going to get away with glamming up like Russell Brand anytime soon, it doesn't work like that, but hey, you might pick up some tips to compliment your style along the way.

Thanks to the world of the internet and highly accessible visual mediums, you can study your idols to your hearts content. Whether it's through their back catalogue of films, books or music, there are plenty of

153

ways to get insight into what makes them tick. Use film footage and live appearances to see what gives them their edge.

Whether you love or hate them, channelling the greatest seducers in history will get you thinking. The added bonus is a refreshed interest in popular culture. There's barely a woman alive who won't be impressed by your celebrity knowledge, especially if you can offer an informed opinion on Cheryl Cole's latest lurve drama! Just don't be going all Zoolander on us!

At the end of this section you will find a list of books and films to kick-start your own personal action/erotic hero film-fest; or at the very least have you studying up on the great seducers, from Errol Flynn to Bogart and Sinatra to name a but a few.

What's all this got to do with flirting? Erm, only everything! It's a reminder that you need to be savvier when it comes to your romantic lives. They do need to be tweaked, tightened and monitored in the same way that our careers and friendships are. It's just plain lazy leaving it to chance. Especially if you have goals that include parenthood and marriage some day; you can't be taking that stuff for granted (I don't care how old you are!). Put simply, in this day and age, it does require thought and planning – if you want a long lasting partnership that is. So if a closer analysis of the Super Seducers provides inspiration to help in your pursuit of an extraordinary life – then bring it on!

### *Zero to Hero...*

Don't ever kid yourself that you can't be the leading man. Just look at superstar rockers Noel Gallagher, Dave Grohl and Gary Barlow – well he's no rocker, but you get my drift. Who knew they could even sing until their leading men went AWOL? By studying the secrets of the old and the new from sportsmen and rock stars to politicians – you'll find out what makes us gals' go potty over their totty.

*Who are your idols and why?*

E.g. Craig Daniels, because he's a legend!

*What characteristics do you best  identify with?*

The strong, silent, macho thing

*Male Order Celeb: In 2011 1,500 UK men voted for what the Ultimate Man should look like and the results were thus:*

✓   Gerald Butler - Face
✓   Brad Pitt - Torso
✓   Matthew McConaughey - Super Toned Body
✓    Jake Gyllenhaal - For Sheer Phwoar Factor!

Now that you've identified the role models that inspire you in the general sense, it's time to identify those whose style appeals to you. Refer to your list of aspirationals and pick out those you just look at and think, '*Whoa!*' Whether it's Paul Newman in the *Colour of Money* or Craig Daniels as 007, and describe the image you admire in as much detail as you can. Think about the changes you need to make to sex up your overall look. Once you've done that, work on tweaking it down to a style that you can call your very own.

Look to the men who are winning the fashion plaudits. Experts in the field of fashion crowned British actor Aaron Johnson as the country's snappiest male dresser in 2010 when he was voted Britain's best dressed man by GQ. Apparently, he personifies the modern British look and style – so there you go!

### High profile dudes who made the grade

✓ Aaron Johnson

✓ Douglas Booth

✓ Nicholas Hoult

✓ Robert Pattinson

✓ Prince Harry

✓ David Furnish

✓ Tom Ford

✓ Alex James

✓ Jenson Button

✓ Bill Nighy

***Flirt-O-Meter: The Good, the Bad and the Ugly of the Super Seducers***

***Russell Brand***: Here you have a bloke who claims to have slept with Kate Moss, so bloomin' hell, he must be doing something right! He may be married now, but before that it was Sun's Serial Shagger of the Year all the way. With that title under his belt, he's clearly got the cred. What's his secret with the ladies? For a start it's his distinctive look, which just like marmite, you either love or hate – but whatever you think of it, it's truly his own. And for those with a penchant for rockstars doused in heroin chic, Brand's nailed it. He's sexy in his own way; all long legs, leather and wild locks, but it's not just his looks that win him the ladies, it's his smarts. Let's look at his Top 5 tactics:

1. His ability to *feminise* himself is his No 1. Secret Weapon. He's in touch with his girly side. He carries on just like a girl: the way he gossips, giggles and drops the dirt on celebs. It makes the ladies drop their defences (and in many cases, that's not all!).

2. He's got a fearless take on dating and flirting. His method is simply to put it out there. He has happily shared his secrets with the *Sun* in the past, and said it's all about acknowledging the moment. He will just come right out and say it:*" Where is the flirting? Are we flirting? Are we enjoying the flirting?"* Masterstroke!

3. He's funny and silly, and always the first to poke fun at himself. Since it's a widely known fact that Brits love anyone who doesn't take themselves to seriously and can have a laugh at themselves, he's made himself a very popular boy!

4. The comedy element is the cherry on top. He's funny as all hell and every girl loves a comedian.

5. Plus, according to Katy Perry, he's no walkover. She says: *"In previous relationships I feel like I've just steamrolled the guy, so it's nice to find someone I can't do that to."*

So where does it all end? Where else but the bedroom of course! Love him or hate him, the man is the master. *Scoreboard: 9/10*

**CLASSIC - *George Clooney***: Clooney's working with A-grade material and has the movie star looks to pull it off. But it's more than that. It's the twinkle in his eye, the greying of the temples, the impeccably tailored suits. He's a complete and utter natural. The fact that he's made it to the age of 50 and never married only makes him more appealing. He's the one who got away. And before you even go there, he's not gay! 10/10

**BAD BOY - *Colin Farrell***: Farrell's appeal lies in those liquid brown eyes, the roguish charm and of course, the Irish accent. It's a wicked combination and enough to makes grown women drool. Scoreboard: 9/10

**STRONG SILENT TYPE - *Daniel Craig***: Two words: Blue Swimmers – that's what most women remember about his Bond debut. This was our cue to go Phwwooooooooooaaaarrr! Because he's fit, and wet. And fit, and wet. Mmm. Oh, and did I mention he's fit and wet? The thing about Craig is that he doesn't have to say a goddamn word. He's got that strong, silent thing down pat. The fact that he rarely gets gossiped about in the press means that he's got the mystery element going on as well. 9/10

**FUNNY MAN - *David Walliams***: You only have to look at the women he's squired to see this guy is a legend when it comes to the almighty art of seduction. It's not that obvious by looking at him, but think about it: he dresses sharply, he's super fit (having swum the Channel), and just like his buddy Brand, he's perfected the art of the non-threat. He's done it by cultivating a light, funny approach which has the effect of making women drop their guard. Once they've dropped their guard, he swoops. Clever, calculated – and all about the comic timing! *Plus he married a real life super model! So he must be good.*

***QUINTESSIANTALLY UNIQUE - Johnny Depp***: There are plenty of Johnny fans who will remain diehard fans forever. He makes a hot dang pirate and he's still the same conventionally gorgeous guy who broke Kate Moss's heart, and for that alone, the man is a legend! Even if we can't quite forgive him for marrying that saucy French tart! 9/10

***SPORTS LEGEND - Lewis Hamilton***: He may be pint sized, but he's ripped and cute as a button. Plus he's super successful with the ladies, which explains how he came to have one of the hottest women on the planet on his arm. Take a bow Pussycat Doll Nicole Scherzinger. In spite of it all, Hamilton still manages to come across as humble. We salute him. 8/10

***OLD SCHOOL ENGLISH GENT - Colin Firth***: Now here's someone who radiates a simmering brand of sex appeal. He really is Mr Darcy personified. Everything about him says integrity, and we love a man with integrity. The Bridget Jones role did much to solidify his place as the nation's heart throb. He's strong, dignified and he simply OOZES English charm. Best of British, chaps! 9.5/10

***MACHO - Hugh Jackman***: What you have here is a modern day caveman who could oh so easily scoop the ladies up with his big manly arms and cradle us against his Tarzan style chest. Drool! He's debonair, dishy and an incredible hunk. Anyone else feeling a bit inadequate now? Needless to say, if I wasn't already taken, he could bowl this maiden over anytime! I'll give him a naughty 9.5/10 for being the man we'd most like to have a naked tickle fight with!

***GEEK - Louis Theroux***: Bespectacled, gangly, skinny, awkward and a prize nerd – hardly the wish-list for the Perfect Boyfriend, but unexpectedly, refreshingly cute!

### Honourable Mentions

*Marco Pierre White* – take a bow Britain's first rock-star chef.

*Javier Bardem*: Style Icon – we salute you!

Strangely attractive *Jack Black* – what is it about fat, funny men?

*Hugh Grant* – he of the floppy fringe and unofficial spokesperson for Hack-gate!

*Barack Obama* – The man. The legend. The charm. Sorry, I couldn't hold myself back there!

*Celeb Quote: Hollywood star Olivia Wilde on Daniel Craig:*
*"He is so fine and he doesn't even know it. He's such a goof, but he has a confidence that allows him to shine In the way that Steve McQueen stole every single scene in The Magnificent Seven, Daniel has that kind of luminosity because of his energy and the kind of saltiness that I think is an important quality of acting. I think that the reason that he redefined Bond is because he has a dirtiness to him. It looks like he has been in bar fights. He's windblown.* (Interesting choice of word usage there: dirty, salty, windblown… it's all very rough 'n' tumble!)

*Hero Vs Zero: Schwarzenegger, the Terminator turned US Governor appeared live on a BBC TV report with Boris Johnson. In spite of being a good twenty years older, Arnie made Boris look flaccid, floppy and old. If you want to look good in a few decades time, then best you find out Arnie's secret (Stop Press: May 2011 - I think we just found out Arnie's secret!)*

# Boys Night In

Show time folks! It's time to organise your own personal movie-fest and watch closely as the romantic leads go about the business of getting it on. The missive is to identify the particular styles at work here. Once you've got a couple of movies, grab a beer, a barrel of popcorn; arm yourself with a pen and pad and focus! Afterwards you will be a natural when it comes to spotting the *SSS: Signature Seduction Styles*.

➢ Paul Newman: *The Colour of Money*

➢ Brad Pitt: *Thelma & Louise*

➢ Humphrey Bogart: *Casablanca*

➢ Richard Gere: *An Officer and a Gentleman*

➢ John Malkovich: *Dangerous Liaisons*

➢ Olivier Martinez: *Unfaithful*

➢ Jack Nicholson: *The Witches of Eastwick*

➢ Steve McQueen: *The Thomas Crown Affair/The Magnificent Seven*

➢ Kevin Spacey: *American Beauty*

➢ Dustin Hoffman: *The Graduate*

➢ Tom Cruise: *Magnolia/Risky Business/Top Gun*

➢ James Mason: *Lolita*

➢ Colin Firth and Hugh Grant: *Bridget Jones*

➢ Jon Hamm: *Mad Men*: A sexy retro TV drama better known as the sexiest thing to ever implode across our televisions.

***Staying In...***

Any of the following books will give you insight into what makes these legendary (and not so legendary) Lotharios tick.

> Lord Byron: *Don Juan*

> The Autobiography of Errol Flynn: *My Wicked Wicked Ways*

> An Unauthorized Biography Of Frank Sinatra: *His Way*

> Jack, the Great Seducer: *The Life and Many Loves of Jack Nicholson*

> Russell Brand: *My Booky Wook*

> Keith Richards: *Life*

> Richard Branson: *Losing my Virginity*

> Lord Alan Sugar: *A Biography of Alan Sugar*

> *Casanova's Memoirs*

For inspirational tales of how these men wooed their women - and lived happily ever after:

> Toby Young: *How to Lose Friends and Alienate People*

> Michael McIntyre: *Life and Laughing: My Story*

***Tackle too Tiny?***

As for the worst flirts in Britain, what about disgraced MP Limp-bit Öpik-Wotsit? If he's not a poster boy for birth control, I don't know what is!

*Planet Geek: Latino stunner Eva Mendes sighs orgasmically when she confesses that she loves a geek – glasses and all – and to be fair, geeks are bang on trend right now. In this age of gadgetry, every girl needs a geek!*

### *Last Hurrah: Summary of Flirt Styles*

A quick recap of the signature styles of the Super Seducers will refresh your memory and prepare you for creating own profile. As you progress through the exercises you will start to find those aspects of flirting that feel instinctively natural to you.

✓ **Colin Farrell**: Signature flirt – Hard and Fast: in your face sexuality

✓ **Russell Brand**: Signature flirt – Cheeky, brash in yer face cockiness

✓ **Sean Penn**: Signature flirt – Tough, tempestuous and passionate

✓ **Brian Ferry**: Signature flirt – International Man of Mystery – and sexy as hell

✓ **Simon Cowell**: Signature flirt – Powerful, arrogant, cocky and charming (in his own weird way)

### *Who do you rate as the Super Seducers and why?*

✓ **Daniel Craig**: Silent, brooding persona

✓ **Russell Brand**: Because he's an outrageous flirt and just doesn't care

✓ **George Clooney**: Because he's timeless, classic lady crack

✓ **David Beckham**: Master of the strong silent type – which on some days can look more baffled and bewildered than sex on a stick. Gotta love him either way though!

### *Now add yours*

1. .....................................................................................

2. .....................................................................................

3. .....................................................................................

### Sex & Movie Star Moments

*"Sex is a momentary itch, love never lets you go."*

**– Kingsley Amis**

*"Sex without love is a meaningless experience, but as far as meaningless experiences go its pretty damn good."*

**– Woody Allen**

*"Remember, sex is like a Chinese dinner. It ain't over 'til you both get your cookie."*

**– Alec Baldwin**

*"How about a drink at my place. No funny business, just full sex."*

**– Hugh Grant, *Bridget Jones***

*"Sometimes you've just got to say what the fuck? and make your move"*

**– Tom Cruise, *Risky Business***

## Sizzling and Saucy Seductresses

Do you know what makes Kelly Brook a very good flirt and Victoria Beckham a very bad flirt? If not, you should. Let's turn to the foxy ladies for tips and clues and study their top-of-the-line-no-poncy bollocks moves. Tune into the female psyche and learn to recognise the Internationally Recognised Signs that tell you they're keen. Information is power after all, especially if you're missing signals left right and centre. Once you've studied how they do it, you'll never need miss another signal again!

The following films offer an insight to the different ways that women 'work it'. Start with the femmes from the Hollywood Age and finish with the contemporary Superflirts. See how they lick their lips and raise their eye-brows oh-so seductively. Watch for volume and repetition – a rapid-fire-machine-gun approach as she goes about dishing out all manner of signs and gestures. Of course you'll be studying the leading men as they kick out the jams as well.

### Warning: These Films Contain Hot Women!

➤ Marlene Dietrich, *Blue Angel*

➤ Greta Garbo, *Camilla*

➤ Rita Hayworth, *Gilda*

➤ Jane Fonda, *Barbarella and Klute*

➤ Faye Dunaway, *Chinatown*

➤ Marilyn Monroe, *How to Marry A Millionaire*

➤ Kathleen Turner, *Body Heat*

➤ Linda Fiorentino, *The Last Seduction*

➤ Drew Barrymore, *Poison Ivy*

### *Babe Watch: Top 10 Superflirts*

- Christina Hendricks: Curvaceous as all hell and commonly described as sex on legs, she oozes old fashioned sex appeal in every sense of the word

- Shakira: She's got it and she flaunts it. Sexy and very predatory

- Rhianna: One word: smokin'!

- Scarlett Johansson: Smouldering in the manner of a serious 40s style screen siren

- Cameron Diaz: Funny, goofy , clever and sexy

- Drew Barrymore: Natural, cheeky and charming

- Nicole Scherzinger: Sexy and strong with a dominatrix vibe going on

- Kelly Brooks: It's pretty obvious

- Cheryl Cole: She's cute, she's tiny – and look she's singing


### *Who Tickles Your Fancy?*

- Jessica Alba

- Abbie Cornish

- Jessica Biel

- Charlize Theron

- Angelina Jolie

- Diane Kruger

- Kirsten Dunst

- Emma Watson

- Pixie Lott or...

- Last but not least...*Ann Widdecombe?*

166

- **Belly Laughs:** Speaking publicly about her past marriages, Katie Price said: *"I am very, very, very, very disappointed with my past marriages."* That's quite a statement from Katie but let me ask you this, where do you rate Miss Katie Price on the Flirt-o-meter and what would you give her out of ten? I'm curious because I've never come across anyone who considered her a flirt – she's a lot of other things, but, a flirt, maybe not...

## Movie Star Oh Movie Star...

Film goddess Kiera Nightly fesses up about the bizarre feedback she gets on the way she looks: *"I have a funny relationship with it because you have some people going, "That's a beautiful face. And others going: That's fucking disgusting."* And they are very vocal about that."

- **Celeb Quote:** Christina Hendricks says: *"Men don't really approach me much, but women do come up and they are flirtatious with me."*
- Hello, where are the MEN?!?!

# What Women Want

While we're on the subject of all things appearances, I want to talk about women's most endearing quality, the thing we pride ourselves on and the thing men love about us most. I am talking of course about our queen size egos. Why NOBODY does ego like us!

I see so much romantic potential smashed because of our egos, and sadly, our insecurities. Worst affected is our self-image which is distorted and over analysed. It doesn't help that we're bombarded with unrelenting images of blindingly beautiful super-models from the moment we tumble out of the womb. Sometimes it seems that everything is based on the way we look – far more so for women than men, don't you agree? Hence why a horrific number of women suffer from eating disorders and self-esteem issues, to the point that if we think our Bum Looks Big In This, we can talk ourselves out of doing anything, or talking to anyone – especially you!

That's a whole can of worms right there. Particularly since we're busy and time poor (because last time I checked, that's what it took to get ahead as a woman). As a result we don't always have the luxury of looking as hot as we'd like. That means we're likely to head out on the town straight from the office without so much as a sideways glance in the mirror. And sometimes, as much as it breaks my heart to say it, we turn up looking like something the cat dragged in. *Shutt Upp!*

The problem there is that women have an unfortunate habit of burrowing themselves away if we're not looking one hundred percent tip-top. We will sit doggedly with our backs glued to the room and pretend we're invisible. Anything rather than show our unadorned faces! I've had so many women turn up to my sessions and beg forgiveness because they haven't turned up with perfect blow-dry or a fully made up face. Even though everyone else thinks they look fine. And if I had a penny for every time I heard the old chestnut: *'I COULDN'T talk to him. I was having a bad hair day'* I'd be a rich woman!

So here's what you need to know, if she is having an off night because she left the house without so much as a slash of Vamp lipstick, then you've got a losing battle on your hands. If she feels unattractive or worse, bloated, she feels unlovable. Yes, women really are that insecure. And if she doesn't feel up to scratch, then she certainly won't think she's good enough for you. Bottom line, she ain't gonna talk to you if she don't feel purdy. Her ego won't let her. Even if she's hot for you; especially if she's hot for you!

So sadly if you do approach whilst she's having a bad face day, she'll probably give you the cool treatment, based purely on the way she looks, or the way she thinks she looks – even if you don't agree. You can't take it personally though. Her self-critique is brutal. General rule of thumb, unless she's done the Wonder Woman transformation from frumpy office-wear into 'stepping out' heels and hair, you're not likely to see any Green Signals coming your way anytime soon. You need to know this is a battle you cannot win.

Which is silly because if you see a girl you fancy, you're not going to grade her out of ten before you make an approach, are you? Surely not! You could care less if she looks less than perfect. That's because men are more forgiving than women which is of course one of the reasons we love you guys. Bless!

Welcome to our fat and fugly day. We all have them and we're entitled to them. The trick is that you'll never know when we're having them but if you get short shift when you try to chat us up, you could consider that it's because we're strung out and feeling like one of the ugly sisters!

## New Kid On The Kop

Now that you've familiarised yourself with the styles of the world's leading Super Seducers, it's time to get your own sorted out. What's yours: Cheeky-chappy? International Man of Mystery? Or good old Mr Reliable?

What is the first impression you'd like to make? e.g.

*I want to come across as confident and self-assured; plus all of the above!*

Describe your personal style?

*I'm a rock n roll guy. I'll never change my style dramatically, but I'm happy to freshen it up if it helps!*

What steps can you take to transform yourself into a guy that women want to talk to?

*Tidy up, work on my presentation. I know my hygiene could be better, so I'll take special care with that..*

What can you do to improve your personal style? *Make more of an effort for starters. My wardrobe is a mess!*

### To summarise let's look at the Key Points

➢ Update wardrobe content and maintenance

➢ Kick-start a grooming regime

➢ Refer to male idols and their style as a source of inspiration

*In a nutshell? Be fit. Be fresh. Be natural. Look good. Smell good.*

### Challenges

✓ Experiment with your style

✓ Get a woman's opinion

✓ Strive to improve your overall look

### KPIs: *Assess your progress*

✓ Are you prepared to experiment with your style? (Y/N)

✓ Will you ask a woman for wardrobe advice?  (Y/N)

✓ How many dress shirts do you have ready for a special date? (1 - 5)

✓ Do you have shiny new shoes ready for a hot date? (Y/N)

✓ Will you do one major thing to improve your overall look? (Y/N)

✓ Is your hair looking the best it can? (Y/N)

✓ Are you prepared to improve your fitness? (Y/N)

**Mantra:** *A competitive spirit will ensure you look good all the time.*

### Checklist

✓ *Enthusiasm*

✓ *Competitive spirit*

✓ *Man-ity, or Vanity*

# Q & A

*Girls always compliment my look, but my mates take the piss. Who should I listen to?*

I think you already know the answer to this one. If the guy's are giving you a hard time, then surely it's because they're jealous don't you think? Even just a tad? And so long as the girls are giving you the thumbs up, who cares?

*Whenever I experiment with my hair, I end up looking like a fool. What to do?*

Rather than putting yourself in the hands of strangers, do some market research. Get opinions from female friends about the style that best suits you. Then ask around for suggestions on where to go. Word of mouth is always best when it comes to tried and true results. Stick to places that others have tried and been happy with the results. Reduce the risk further by taking photos and asking for a consultation before the cut so you can be perfectly clear about what you want.

*I wear head-to-toe black most of the time because I've been told it suits me, but more and more I feel like I blend into the background. Should I change my style to stand out more?*

There's nothing wrong with wearing black as your main colour provided it's a style statement and not a reflection of your state of mind. Jazz it up with coloured accessories like belts and bright sneakers to bring your outfit to life and stop you from fading into the background.

*Which muscles do women like the most?*

Body type preference is such a personal thing. So in the same way that you might be a 'boob' or a 'bum' man, women have her preferred body parts as well. Maybe it's the abs, the butt, or for some women, a muscular forearm or a set of toned calves. Or it might be a bulging set of 'builder's

173

biceps' that lures her (or she could find them the ultimate turn-off). The best bet is to emphasise your favourite body parts and find out that way.

*I have a hairy back and it's never really bothered me, but I've just started seeing someone and I'm worried she'll hate it. Should I wax it?*

There's nothing wrong with having a hairy back and there's no need to be ashamed. It's just testosterone at the end of the day, it's not like you've got 3 penises. Rather than assume she's going to hate it, why not tell the lady in question – before she encounters it in real life. Who knows, she may not be as put off as you think. There's a danger in getting it waxed without mentioning it because as soon as it starts to grow back, you'll be rumbled anyway. It might be easier to just 'fess up now!

# Step 4. Building Your Dating Profile

## Psycho Sexual Admin

So here we are then...with you, the leading man, in the starring role. You have a central part, *the* central part. The only thing that matters from now on, is that you enjoy all this. If you genuinely get a kick out of chatting and flirting, and you can do that without being a sex-pest, then you're halfway there. But if you find it all a bit of a struggle, and you see girls as some kind of three-headed alien life-form, there are ways to improve your situation – so long as you're up for the challenge. It's never too late to learn the tools and rules of how to charm someone and make them laugh. We're talking about the ability to come across as a nice bloke with a lovely smile. It's not that complicated.

Thanks to the training courses and classes I run, I come across all kinds of girls – beautiful, bashful, baffling and complicated – mainly complicated girls. What I've found in dealing with these complex creatures (besides having the job *you* want ☺) is that you never know what you're dealing with until you get to know someone... But generally speaking, when it comes to what Her Royal Hotness is looking for in a man, it's pretty basic.

You should be confident, charming and courteous, someone who makes her think: *"Cor, I wouldn't mind a bit of that!"* To be a cool guy who makes everyone laugh. Once others meet you, they will want to get to know you more. You will have good taste...in films, food, fashion – and you will love puppies and kittens. Every woman will secretly wish she was with you because you don't take yourself too seriously...and because you put the fun in mental – you're fundamental! Mostly because you're not scared of, you know, the emotional stuff...but mainly because you're sweet and considerate and you know how to make us feel like The Only Girl In The World. In your own quirky way, with all your bumpy imperfections – you are perfect. And perfectly entitled to the most whopping romance of the century, which is of course why you're here.

This is where you knuckle down and focus on what you're looking for. If it is simply that you have a great job, great friends and great family, but there's just one thing missing – and that is a W-O-M-A-N – someone with whom you can have a giggle and a bit of slap and tickle; someone who you can take away on mini-breaks – then I get that. But, rather than feeing all sad about your WFS: *Woefully Freakin' Single* status, you might find you benefit from doing some self-analysis. So, let's take a step back.

In the following pages I've set some assignments and tasks which can be carried out in whichever way works best for you, but I strongly advise you do them, however cringe-worthy they feel. And yes, I know that wading through self-reflective work can be excruciating, but I for one, would be very interested to know how you get on. Certainly if you came to see me for a face-to-face consultation at Dating HQ, it's the very first thing I would ask you to do.

The fantastic thing about doing this stuff is that by writing things down in black and white, you're giving yourself a chance to see what's going on – or what's going wrong. Looking back will allow you to see more clearly, those instances where you've hit the jackpot, and the dividends have been amazing. But more importantly where you crashed and burned. From there, you will be better positioned to figure out the reasons behind it and hopefully avoid any repeat sucker-punches.

Moreover, it's a good way to spot negative patterns with past relationships in a bid to steer clear of them in the future. To do this successfully, you need to come from a position of strength and focus on what you've got to offer. We'll start with how you perceive yourself, right now at this point of your life. This is important stuff since what you believe to be true about yourself, is a by-product of the way you come across to others. It might not be the easiest thing to do, but rest assured, the deeper you look and the more you squirm – the better.

It doesn't help that life in the 21$^{st}$ Century is tough – really tough. We live in busy, overcrowded cities filled with uncertainty and dark forces. The population of singles is bigger than ever before. Based on numbers alone, the pursuit of romance should be easier, but it's not. That's because we've lost faith in one of the most elemental things – trust in human beings. I'm writing this literally days after the British riots. What the f*** has happened to our society? And how does that impact on our romantic lives? As if it wasn't hard enough already!

Added to that, a reported one in every two marriages in this country ended in divorce in recent years – one in every two!! Getting together and having the happy ever after is not the most straightforward thing, and it's not easy for anyone. No matter whether you're single, married or in a relationship. As Chezza Cole said: *'You've got to fight, fight, fight, fight for this love.'*

And who really knows what stops us from being the dating demon we'd love to be. We're only human and we all sabotage ourselves at some level, some of us more than others. If you have a habit of screwing up all the great opportunities that come your way, and you're able to admit to it, you need to unearth the reasons and deal with them. There's no room for persecution complexes here. If you've got a victim mentality you've got to lose it. Before you can lose it, you've got to figure out why you've got it. Repeat after me: *'I am NOT an emotional terrorist!'*

But hang about, since this step is all about shaking up your confidence, overcoming confusion conspiracy theories, and getting to the stage where you're ready to step out on some practice dates, we'll need to address a few preliminary issues, all about you. So before we get down to the nitty-gritty of what to look for, and how to respond when it comes to the flirting femmes, it's time to figure out how best to manage your expectations, otherwise how else will you get on top of them?

Likewise if you are naturally reluctant to open up about your life, and the idea of sharing your shortcomings is not something that comes naturally, then I'd like to ask you to stop and have a think about who you can trust as a confidante. If there is someone that comes to mind, consider talking to them about those areas in which you could do with some guidance. If not, consider getting a professional option; there are crisis lines available for this kind of thing available 24/7. We all need a different perspective from time to time and a second opinion provides just that. It's nothing to be ashamed of. Knowledge is power. It's also a good starting point. But enough of the love fest, let's go in search of a little self-knowledge!

# Romance Resume

A key part of the psycho-sexual reinvention is to draw up a Romantic CV – a précis of your dating experience if you like. The point is that sometimes you need to look back in order to move forward. By summarising the details of your PRH: Personal Romantic History, you stand to gain a better understanding of yourself, a good point from which to set your learning compass. It's also a way to kick-start the self-analysis and learn a thing or two about yourself, your philosophies and principles, and the way you come across to the world. Or perhaps more importantly how you *could* come across if you upgraded your psycho-sexual skills. Consider this your personal mind-map from which you join the dots to get to the next spot.

And when you think about it, why wouldn't you take a strategic approach to romance? You almost certainly didn't depend on random chances to get where you are with your career. I'll bet that wherever field you are in and whatever job you're doing right now, it's the result of intelligently plotted strategies, tactics and hard work. Eh? So of course it makes sense to adapt this approach to kick-start your love life.

Let's start with your romantic situation, what's happening with it right now, as in today? Are you seeing anyone? A FWB: Friend with Benefits perhaps? Or an old flame whose clutches you can't escape? Is there someone on whom you have a crush – nothing more, nothing less? Or, have you been loveless and looking for so long, that frankly you're over it?

Now ask yourself this: What's the big attraction for a relationship? Company? Companionship? Access to cuddles 24/7? Or is it the thought of sex for breakfast, lunch and tea? Moreover, does the lack of sex make you feel dizzy? If so, what are the reasons you crave sex so badly? Is it simply to fulfil a biological need? Or is it more about the inevitable ego-boost? Does sex translate to emotion in your world? What about your self-worth? Do you think that having a woman by your side will validate you and your life will magically become more interesting and fun?

If that is the case, you might want to rethink it.

Think about what you've learnt about yourself during the course of past relationships, and those things you'd like to change. Now ask yourself where you see yourself in the romantic stakes? Where would you like to be in the next six months, twelve months and beyond? Are you ready to identify and build upon your weaknesses? If the answer is yes, then you have to be clear about the areas you need to work on. The next step is to record your romantic history and the repeat patterns that resulted in destructive outcomes.

In identifying your goals and going after them, you need to access your confidence reserves. Since we're speeding towards our very own 2012 Olympics, let's look at how the Olympian superstars do it. Clearly every waking moment focused on the key goal. Every breath they take and every choice they make, from what they eat, to the hours they sleep, what they drink and how they think, is motivated by the overwhelming desire to win. In order to get to the stage where your every choice is governed by the end goal, we need to look at self-esteem and self-confidence, both of which are crucial to the end result.

## The C Word: Topping Up Your Confidence

*"Oh, just be yourself and everything will be fine!"* Is what we hear from the experts when it comes to how to manage make or break situations. But it's hard to be "yourself" when you're in a blind panic isn't it? And how are you supposed to be confident *and* be yourself at the same time? As anyone who's been on the wrong end of a bad job interview or the date from hell can testify, it can be tricky. So what is self-confidence? And how can you apply it to the 'be yourself' theory?

The amount of self-confidence you have is a direct link to how successful you see yourself. If you have made bad decisions and acted in ways where you have been unsuccessful, it normally follows that you will feel less confident. If your confidence has been battered, it will affect the way you approach things. Perhaps there was a time when you went for jobs only to be rejected again and again. If that happened to you, it's likely that after a time you started doubting yourself. You probably beat yourself up and blamed yourself for every little thing that went wrong in the interview process. Gradually it niggled away at you and started to eat away at your confidence. After a while things built up to the point where you began to carry those fears around everywhere with you, effectively sabotaging yourself – and not just in the job situation, but every situation, whether it was making new friends or chatting up women.

Self-confidence is your belief in your skills and abilities to *do* things and kick goals. It's fed by those things you do – whether that's sports prowess, business acumen or your ability to clean-up on the dance-floor. It can be measured by the way you feel in your day-to-day life. Are you Happy, Grumpy, Dopey or Bashful? Are you grateful for the highs you experience and glad to be alive? Or are you one of these people who only gets worked up about the stuff that really pisses you off, and forgets about the good stuff? Or worse, is never satisfied with what you see in the mirror? If that's the case, and your emotional range is restricted to a range of

182

disappointment, hostility and self-loathing – and we've all been victims of from time to time – then you need to work on building your self-esteem.

It's important to differentiate between self-confidence and self-esteem because while your self-confidence may appear strong on the surface, underneath, your self-esteem could be in tatters. In other words, even though you might feel perfectly fine with what you've 'achieved' in life, it doesn't mean a thing if you don't feel good from the 'inside'.

Self-esteem provides the foundations and feeds your self-confidence. It's how you *feel* about yourself on a deeper level, or how much self-worth, or self-love you feel. In order to have a healthy tank of self-esteem, you need a strong sense of self-worth. That means you need to top up in those areas which make you feel loved and cared for, and tap into the good stuff, the stuff that is real. That could mean resolving a situation which has resulted in you feeling isolated, or simply reaching out to family and friends, or somebody that you trust.

**It's like the T-Shirt says:** *"It's what's inside that counts."*

## Alpha Dog Vs the Shy Guy

When I talk about self-confidence, I'm not talking about your personality type. It's got nothing to do with whether you're a brash, brazen shouty-mouth type, or the shy type. What matters is how confident you feel within YOURSELF and how you project that.

And so what if you're shy? Just because somebody is louder than you, or they 'act' more confident, it doesn't mean they are. Insecurities have a way of affecting our personas, the image we put out to the world, with the outcome that we often keep our real selves, hidden behind a façade.

If you're hiding behind a mask and pretending to be someone you're not, or dishing out a constant stream of wisecracks and dripping in sarcasm banter, eventually that will come across. Likewise if you genuinely believe in yourself and you are self-assured, regardless of whether you say or do the wrong thing, then that will come across as genuine confidence.

We've all met the *Oh-So-Confident Sammy Suave* guy. He's the one who fancies himself the ladies man and likes to think he's all clued up about this seduction lark. He is dripping in attentiveness while he flatters senselessly and attempts to charm the ladies pants off. His alligator grin is always at the ready and he's poised to attack. His primed like a beady-eyed hawk watching for the signals. He automatically assumes every woman is waiting for him to hit on her. He can be very cocky and convincing to get his point across, or VERY, VERY LOUD.

Why is it always the turkey-cocking guys who use arrogance to cover insecurities? Arrogance doesn't equate to self assurance, if anything, it makes him look like a greedy, needy prat who was bullied at school. The louder Mr. Shouty Crackers, the bigger the turn off. So don't be falling for the widely sprouted theory that women prefer Alpha Dogs, it's not the case at all. Most women are clued up enough to know that the OTT guys, the players and the el-smootho's, come with their own set of challenges. If he's sniffing around them like a dog on heat, he's probably doing the same with everyone in a skirt.

### *What Makes Sammy Suave Stand Out In A Crowd?*

✓ The relentless obnoxious remarks
✓ The incessant ogling at our breasticles and pawing at our clothes
✓ The 'Come Party On My Face' T-shirt
 *Charlie Sheen, stand aside!*

Then there's his opposite number: The Shy Guy, with his cute, crooked smile. In conversation he blinks rapidly as he wonders what the hell-o to say. In the heat of the moment he may be pathologically clueless especially when it comes to making a move. To make matters worse, he might be licking his wounds from the last violent apprehension he got when he so much as smiled at someone and was bitch-slapped so hard and so fast, he swore he'd never go there again. Understandably he's nervous about making an approach again. Ever!

Let's say you're that shy guy, not so extreme, but enough that you're lurking in the back stalls avoiding the spotlight. You might be a lightweight when it comes to verbal delivery and blowing your own trumpet, but in reality, you're the one with the backbone of steel, the silent but deadly dynamo, the elusive powerhouse – they say it's the quiet ones you have to watch. If that's the case, you've got to find a way to let your personality shine through – shy or not!

I'm not one to underestimate the debilitating effect shyness can have, I know only too well it can be crippling. But if you can manage to overcome your nerves enough to have a laugh, and open up to us, we won't mind at all. There's nothing off-putting about your mild mannered personality, so long as your shyness isn't mistaken for aloofness or arrogance. The secret is to not to let it become such a big deal. We will only put you in the too hard basket if you are so painfully shy that you can't work up the courage to talk to us. Especially if you are so bedazzled by our sassy looks and charm that you fail to make any sense; and strange, muffled noises come out of your mouth in place of words. That could be tricky.

If you're shy, then by all means be shy, but *own it*. Don't let your shyness stop you from living your life and having a laugh. If you the moment is right, and your chemistry is crackling but the words aren't happening, just put it out there. Be honest. Tell us you're having a Frank Spencer moment and feeling a bit erm, awkward. Tell us it's not your thing to be out and about chatting up the ladies. Where's the harm? If anything we'll appreciate it because it shows us that you're not a Del boy, a dodgy geezer or a conman.

### *'Slow And Steady Wins The Race'* Said Mr. Tortoise

Many women, particularly successful, sassy women, sometimes known as Alpha Women, go for the quiet guys. That's because opposites attract. We're not necessarily looking for someone whose personality mirrors our own. The more outgoing we are, the more likely we are to favour a low-key partner, or vice versa.

I can't speak for everyone, but if we see ourselves as a real go-getter, we might not exactly be over excited by the prospect of being with someone with the same go-getting characteristics as ourselves, that can be exhausting! Especially if we've already had the experience of being with someone just like us, and found it to be the most god-awful thing ever! And yes, I am talking from experience. That's the best thing about past relationships – they show us what we *don't* want!

I'm reminded here of an ancient episode on *Seinfeld*, where Jerry got engaged to the character played by Janeane Garofalo. Her character was the identikit female version of him which is why he fell for her hard. It started out all peachy, but then it got really creepy and the two of them ended up freaking each other out. Just like in real life!!

186

Given the choice, we might well find we prefer to be with someone from whom we can learn new tricks. Someone who can help us stop and smell the roses and offer a life view refreshingly differently to ours. That's exciting! So don't think that just because you don't display your manliness in the traditional hairy-bummed-ape way, that women won't appreciate you. Well not all women obviously, but the sensitive, intelligent ones – clearly I'm including myself here.

That's my cue to get up on my pedestal and shout out to anyone who'll listen, it's the guys sitting on the side-lines, in reserve, they're the good guys, THEY'RE THE KEEPERS. So for all the shy guys who think they're not good enough, loud enough, or ballsy enough – this one's for you. At the end of the day if someone doesn't like you for who you are, they can sod off!

But suppose you secretly wish you were a bad boy because *'that's what women want?'* Or so you've heard. Do you bemoan the fact that your friends are always saying, *"You're too nice."* Are you inclined to agree? Well be that as it may, you are simply being yourself. You can't go changing your personality to become a cliché of what women *supposedly* want! That would be destructive and dangerous. And stupid!

If high-school taught you nothing except the idea that the bad guys are the cool guys, the popular guys, and as a result, the guys who get all the sex, then of course there will be times when you've felt your personality was never going to cut it. Particularly if you weren't into games and the whole, *'treat 'em mean keep 'em keen'* carry on. But whatever your personality, there's more to you than the jack the lad good-egg, we've all got a dark side. And, here's the thing – the bad boy stuff is all urban myth. It's complete and utter fantasy; a romantic cliché. I'm not saying that women don't go through their bad boy phase, of course we do. It's exciting and naughty. But then we grow out of it. And we grow up. And want a good man. A real man. A man like you.

187

### Finding The 'Essence' Of You

Think about what drives your personality the next time you find yourself in one of those situations where you're acting spontaneously and passionately, and genuinely having a good time; those times when you feel funny and likeable and popular. Maybe it's when you're with family or friends or both – the point is you're being YOURSELF. You're doing those things you feel passionate about, or that come naturally to you. It's very different to those times you find yourself 'pretending' to have a good time, but inside you're stifled by self-monitoring. Or when you're acting the way you THINK you should act – not the way you would act naturally.

It's when we drop the façade, or the 'act' that all is revealed – and it's our essence that shines through. That's the stuff you need to siphon to make your personal life go through the roof. That's what I mean when I say, *'Just be yourself'.*

### Patterns from your Past

It helps to look at past relationships and the way you feel about the outcomes. Have your past mistakes taught you how to spot Li'l Miss Trouble at a hundred paces? Can you spot the recurring themes and put them into words? What about your impulse to enter into destructive relationships? Do you still get reeled in every time you see a hot babe in a *'Wanna Be My Sex Slave?'* T-Shirt? And no matter how hard you try, are you unable to kick your 'bad girl' addiction? In other words, are you likely to walk back into the same disaster zones?

Think back to your first proper heartbreak, that time when you were momentarily crippled in the carnage. Who broke your heart? Where is she now? Can you move on?? Have you moved on? What's happened since? Are you over it? Or fuelled by bitterness and confusion? Do you blame yourself for the failure of a past relationship? Or absolutely despise your psychotic knife wielding bitch of an ex – and blame her completely? Or could it be that a busted heart and a few months, or years, of scraping by has made you humble and more human? Perhaps you're older and wiser, and better at looking things? Do you see the bigger picture and appreciate how the experience bought another dimension into your life?

That brings us to the current day. What's holding you back in your love life right now? Is it your ex, your work, your weight, your financial situation? Whatever the answers, you need to sort it. Whether that's making your peace with the previous relationship, or going out for a dirty old rebounder – you owe it to yourself.

In order to get what you want, you need to know what it is. Consider the kind of relationship you're looking for. Is it a sweet and soppy long-term romance? Or simply something to tide you over until your next move, whether that's between cities, jobs or even countries? Are you rebounding so hard that you're only up for Ms Right For Now – a dirty one-night stand at worst, a fast and furious fling at best. Whatever it is, say it out loud.

### *You Can't Always Get What You Want*

What do you see when you look back at your romantic past? Were there ever any instances where you had more success with the women on whom *you were less keen?* More so than the successes you've had with women you pursued really hard? If the answer is yes, that's because typically the more we fancy someone, the less keen they are. And vice-versa. It's just the way it is. There is such a thing as wanting something too much. When we want something SO BADLY that we'll just DIE if we don't get it – we tend to screw it up.

Likewise if you are desperate for someone to love you with every inch of their body – it's a turn off. Desperation is never attractive. If there is pure terror behind that fixed smile, it will show. That's why it's a good policy to keep your options open and be more relaxed about things! The more easy come, easy go we are, the more we attract good into our lives.

# What Makes You A Good Catch?

In order to unearth the billion and one reasons that make you such a great catch, you need to work on your USP – Unique Selling Points. It's time to put your head down for some hardcore market analysis in order to showcase your best sellers. But first, how do you gauge if you're a good catch? Moreover, if you're not convinced of your 'catch-ability' how on earth are you going to convince anyone else? These are the questions that YOU need to answer. And there's no time like the present. We are going to market the absolute hell out of you.

My big brother used to say that guys just want a girl who really liked them. And it's the exactly the same with girls. But, if you're looking for an awe-inspiring woman, you need to be pretty awe-inspiring yourself. And you have to spell it out, because here's the thing, you can punch above your weight all you like, so long as you've got the confidence. In other words, if you're going to up the wager, you've got to up the weaponry, and you need to back it up. You've got to think in terms of your best qualities – your most saleable qualities. You've got to grab your audience and draw them in. You've got to be out there wowing them with a capital 'W'!

So if you think that just like Britain's funny man, David Walliams you are a clear candidate for a stunning super model girlfriend, then you need to ask yourself – why? What makes you the best boyfriend material in Britain? What is your main draw-card, your secret weapon, your women's kryptonite – your lady crack?

Think about the parts that make up the sum of you. Are you brilliantly gifted, funny, clever, successful, bookish, powerful, rich – or just incredibly hot? Whatever it is, you need to be clear about it. If it turns out you haven't won any Godlike Genius Awards lately – no matter, so long as you're not a sex offender or a war crimes fugitive, you'll be fine. Just play up the stuff you're good at.

# Mind Candy

What is it that *others* like about you? I realise that reeling off your best qualities can be easier said than done since everyone is so stingy with compliments these days. As a result as we blossom into adults and forget what makes us so unique and loveable; whether that's our cheeky smile, profound head of hair, or kissable lips. But, that's all going to change.

Think back to every compliment you've ever had. Go back in time as far as you can and dig around in the recess of your mind. Once you've found them, jot those bad boys down. These are the things that make you unique, that define you and make you the individual you are today. Use them to help you focus on the positives. Too much man potential is wrecked because of insecurities, especially those based around physical attributes. It doesn't matter whether you've got acne or you're overweight – we've all got something we hate about ourselves. There's no point beating yourself up about your shortcomings, the trick is not to dwell on it. What is it the bible says? Accept those things you cannot change...

Personally speaking, I'm not going to beat myself up about not having supermodel looks. I'm happy to study the women I admire for inspiration, but I'm confident enough within myself that I don't depend on my looks. If anything, I think that truly beautiful girls are disadvantaged because they can become dependent on their looks and forget to develop a personality. *Miaow!* But, I digress, back to you...

If you've been getting compliments about your smile from the age of five, know that you still have that cute smile and flash it at every opportunity! All too often I coach men who sit with the most solemn expression, and then, when they finally relent and crack a smile, I see a whole different person. Their face lights up and their eyes shine – it's like some kind of magic. So be sure to include every shiny, happy, nice thing anyone has ever said to you – even if it was after you spiked their skinny latte. Joke people!!

Describe what makes you a decent and lovable bloke. And be honest! It's one thing to embellish the truth, and of course everyone likes to put themselves in the most positive light, but don't take so much creative licence so that the truth is no longer recognisable! You should be able to reel off your top three strengths and weaknesses right off the bat. And don't think this is just for the dating arena, it's handy for job interviews as well; these topics are always up there with recruiters' favourite questions:

***Complete:*** **I'm a great catch because...** My last girlfriend said I was. That was before she dumped me!! But that was more about her than me. Because I'm a good guy and I work hard and I'm fun to be around!

## Top 5 Strengths?

Great sense of humour

I can chat to most people pretty well

I 've been known to be persuasive

I'm creative

And passionate about life

## Weaknesses

I sometimes drink too much

I mumble!

I'm easily put off if something looks 'too hard

I'm easily distracted

I lose my nerve

## *How can you build on the weaknesses?*

E.g. By making a massive effort!

Socialising more

Building up my confidence

Liking myself more!

Going out more

Getting in touch with old friends

Going back to the gym!

## *What do you like most about your character?*

✓   Determined

✓   Creative

✓   Great with kids and animals!

## **What do you like the least?**

✓   Health issues

✓   Bad financial situation

✓   My job!

## **What can you improve in the short term?**

**Write down a few words that best describe you:**

### *Who Am I?*

I'm 26

I'm single.

I recently moved away from home to a new city.

I miss home. But I LOVE being here!

The opportunities are amazing. But it's been a hard slog

I've paid for it in the most unexpected ways. Like making my chances of romance harder!

But I would like to be in a long term relationship. And I'm working on it.

I have something of a weakness for Essex style tanned brunettes, I would love to cop off with Franzy from work, but she's not looking all that interested!

**Now you do it!**

# Baggage

If insecurities are affecting you to the point where you're too terrified to make an approach, because frankly, you've been down that road before and it wasn't pretty – you've got to make a decision to let go of the past. Perhaps you haven't had the opportunity to deal with some major trauma or another, possibly one that you've held onto for years. If that's the case and it's still lurking in the background, silently haunting you, you need to make a pledge to deal with it. Because otherwise, how are you supposed to get off with someone new, when you're inwardly haunted by the ghosts of heartbreak and grief?

We all know the importance of moving on, just as we know that too much time spent in victim mode can affect our personalities. But there is a tendency to ignore it or brush it under the carpet. Often we kid ourselves into believing that we're over a past relationship, whether it was an ill-fated marriage, a fling gone bust, or unrequited lust. Although sometimes what we believe to be true, and the reality, are two very different things. This is the time to confront your past, deal with the crap and make a commitment to let go of any negative reminders – both physical and emotional.

The challenge is to lose the baggage. And by baggage, I'm not talking about the carry-on type; I'm talking about the stuff that keeps you awake at night. The torrid details of the ill-advised one night stand. The negative energy spent wondering did you jump or were you pushed? The shame of knowing that you were being screwed by your ex, in more than one sense of the word.

Then, in the wee small hours of the darkest night when you lie there with your eyes wired open and your mind churning – acknowledge it. And rather than tossing and turning, get up and deal with it. Grab a pen and paper and spew it all out. Then, once you're done, put it away somewhere safe, go back to sleep and deal with it in the cold light of day. You might be shocked by what you read back, but at least you'll know what's going on in your head. By doing this you will be better positioned to sort out the most important thing right now – your priorities.

Wow, that was heavy. Let's lighten the mood and turn our attention to something more fun. Strap yourselves in and let's talk about what kind of woman you fancy.

***Sing Along****: Join in for the rousing chorus of the Foo Fighters' 'Best of You' and ask yourself if someone was, is, or ever has been getting 'The best, the best, the best, the best of you?' And if no-one is, ask yourself how you can make that happen!*

# Fancy a Type?

How good is your radar when it comes to picking the right girl? Or should the question be, do you even have radar? Maybe you are bamboozled by beauty and too quick to dismiss the warning signs? If I was to ask about your type, what would you say and how would you describe her? Or, do you even have a type? For the record, I don't recommend it. In fact anyone who has a particular type and sticks to it is missing out on a whole world of opportunity. Nonetheless for the purpose of the exercise, let us continue.

Assuming that you do have a type, have you had any experience with your fantasy woman? What I'm trying to find out is whether there is any basis to your type, or if it is nothing more than a smoke and mirrors concoction of the feminine qualities you *imagine* you would like?

If that's the case, is there some deep-seated psychological reason that you only fancy the kind of woman found exclusively on Page 3 of the *Sun*? Or do you hanker for a happy-go-lucky homemaker and housekeeper? Maybe your fantasy bird is a high-flying overachiever, someone with whom you see yourself carving out a turbo charged life? Or maybe not...

The point is to think about the characteristics of your dream girl, and ask yourself, honestly, if they are they compatible with your own. Forget about her check-list for the moment, and think about the deal-breakers that make up your list? What does it take for wonder woman to fit the bill and tick your boxes? Is it enough that she is funny and cute and genuine and she has a nice smile – plus she likes you?

All too often we chase after something that's unattainable and highly desirable, and then when reality hits, it's like, yikes! *Fit hits the shan!* It's not what we expected, or what we hoped it would be. But sometimes we have to experience the absolute worst-case scenarios in order to take away the most valuable lessons. That's what stops us from making the same mistakes again.

## Wing-Women & Chemistry...

Does your sister or platonic gal-pal know that you're pining to meet a lady? Because if they don't they should. In fact, the more people who know, the merrier. You never know who might be able to lend a hand on the matchmaking front. Or not? Either way you need to put some thought into attracting more female company in your life for many reasons, but mainly because it's healthy. It's also practical. You want to spend enough time with women so that when someone lush comes along, you'll be completely natural and relaxed. Being with your female friends should feel as comfortable as being with one of your mates.

This is easier if a good portion of your existing friends are women. It's a no-brainer If you grew up in a houseful of girls, but it's a little trickier if you didn't; nor does it help if you went to an all-boys school, especially if it resulted in you growing up feeling tense around women. Until you start to view women as normal people who make up half the population, you'll find it hard to relax around them. That's why you need to go out and forage for some new female friends – not just for dating purposes – but because it's nice having someone around who can champion your single pursuits. The technical name for it is wing-woman. But I don't think that concept works over here, it's just so American.

Professional wing-women are big business in America where they're hired out for big bucks. The point is to show other women that you're the kind of guy who has cool women in your life. Presumably that gets their interest because, hey, you must be a pretty happening guy. That's how it works in theory. And some guys swear by it, but I'm not convinced. That's because if you don't know what you're doing it can backfire spectacularly. I just think it's better to find some platonic gal pals to spend time with.

Who will you enlist for the 'feminine point of view'? Is there a friend of a friend, or a friend of a relative, or an old school pal? If no-one springs to mind immediately, then get on the case and make a pact to get in touch with all the girls you know. There's bound to be someone from your past, most likely someone you've not had contact with for ages? Whether they're old school friends, workmates, acquaintances or legacy friends, just shoot them off a quick email or text. Better still, give them a call if you're comfortable to do so, and see where they're at. It can't hurt. They may be unresponsive in which case nothing lost, nothing gained. Or, they might be going through the exact same thing as you, and have a shortage of opposite sex friends to hang out with, in which case, you meet up for a pint, compare notes and who knows, you could be in for a pleasant surprise. You know the drill, suck it and see. The thing about opposite sex friends is that things have a habit of getting complicated – sometimes very quickly. Treat your female friendships with the platonic respect they deserve until you have reason to suspect that there's the potential for more. Having chemistry is one clue...

Chemistry is a funny thing, and it appears in many guises. Often it's as simple as the sensation we get when we're having a laugh with someone special. But for chemistry to really happen, it takes two people to be tuned in and attracted on a billion levels. It's not enough that she finds you attractive – it takes a lot more than that.

Chemistry is the clang of a million bells and whistles going off at precisely the same time. It's the shyness of the smile, the glow of the cheeks, the tantalising looks that last just a moment too long. It's that *ping!* you get when she touches your arm, the *jolt!* when she accidentally brushes your knee. It's the *click and the whirr!* of something extraordinary that happens when she smiles at you. It's the confidence with which you lean in towards her, without even thinking. It's physical. It's physiological. It's psychological. And you can't make it happen. It's either there or it's not. If you've got a pretty strong feeling it's there – then you'd be a fool not to act on it. Which brings us to...

# The Friend Zone

She's a single woman. You're a single man. She's your drinking buddy, your ultimate fantasy woman, your long-time crush. She's always smiling and laughing, which could mean everything, or nothing. You get along like a house on fire and she seems to like you, so, what's the problem?

The problem is that you've become her mate. And now you can't get past the Friend Zone!

Which to be honest, that's an entire other book right there, because this is one massive, sprawling hell of a topic, and there's not nearly enough space to deal with it thoroughly here. Nevertheless I've included a very broad suggestion in the hope that it sets you in the right direction, because god knows, we've all been bitten by the Friend Bug.

*The Scenario:* You make a new friend and right off the bat you fancy her; or you get closer to an old friend, and all of a sudden, you start to feel all peculiar around her. Either way there's this hot girl, and you're trying desperately to rocket things out of the Friend Zone. Hanging out with her is always so effortless and such a pleasure, apart from when you have too many pints and get horny and she doesn't know you're secretly scoping her out.

When you're around this wanton woman, your imagination goes into overdrive, as you dream up every possible scenario in a bid to get her attention. You're desperate to make a move and want for nothing more than to throw yourself at her. You think romantic thoughts and wish you could just come out and woo her with wine, flowers and passionate trysts. You rack your brain to come up with the ultimate Grand Gesture to blow her tiny little mind, but, there's so much at stake. So much can go wrong. You're terrified of making a fool of yourself, and who can blame you? Standing over your left shoulder is the Almighty Wall of Rejection. *Dum-dum-dum-dummmm!* This is one bullet you want to dodge.

And how are you meant to know if she fancies you? What do you look for and how can you tell...? When you see her you kiss her on both cheeks and search her eyes for clues, but find nothing. *Maybe she's interested, maybe she's not. You think she's interested. She acts interested.... Nah she's not interested! She's just being nice. You're not even sure if she's spoken for. You don't think she is, but maybe she is... Yes she is. No she's not. You're convinced you've read this all wrong. Or have you?* It's so confusing!

At this point, there are basically two choices: the Direct Approach – only for the very brave, or the Indirect Approach. If you choose to go Direct, there are countless ways to do it.

You may boldly choose to make your thoughts known by sending a note, or a bunch of flowers, or you might serenade her outside her bedroom window. Otherwise, you might just come right out and tell her... or you just jolly well lurch yourself at her if that's your fancy.

If your plan is to go the direct route and seduce her by doing all those things you've read about – getting her out for a drink and setting the scene by acting all friendly and familiar and asking her lots of questions and telling her jokes and being funny, no, hilarious – with the hope that at the end of the night you will look her in the eye, hold her hands in yours and tell her you are absolutely crazy about her. At which point she will look at you sweetly and smile...

And she will not say, "*I just want to be friends."*
But of course you must be prepared for her saying that.

Aaaaargh!!!!!!!!!!!!!!!!!!!!!!!!!!!!!!!!!!!!!!!!!!!!!!!!!!!!!!

"*I respect your honesty. I also hate you for it*". You scream into your beer. And then you cry. Tears, just like a girl and throw yourself on the ground and fling your arms and legs in the air.

You took the plunge and asked the question. The answer wasn't the one you wanted, but hey, at least you know the score. If you don't ask you don't get. There's no need for histrionics. You didn't do anything wrong, you just took her by surprise and she wasn't thinking of you in that way at that time…or maybe she needed some time to think about it. Whichever way you look at it though, the cat is out of the bag. That's the thing about the Direct Approach – you do risk everything.

So, before you act, perhaps it's better to weigh it all up and fast forward to the worst case scenario. The question you need to ask yourself is whether the friendship will survive if things don't go as planned? Even worse, will you have to face her at work tomorrow?

Naturally it's a case by case situation and it depends on a billion variables, and how close the two of you are; but, if you want to test the waters without blowing it, your best bet is to find a way to be subtle, but not so subtle that she doesn't get it – and go for the Indirect Approach. It's not so different to the Indirect Approach except that it doesn't have the heavy ending. I should preface it by saying that this approach is only effective if your crush is someone you know well enough that you can get her out for a drink or a coffee…

And from there it's pretty straight forward. All you're doing is creating an opportunity to have a chat, and the more normal it is, the better. Don't deviate too far from what the two of you would normally do together. Keep things as low-key as possible. If you typically have coffee together, then use that time to test the waters; if you regularly have drinks together, even better.

Prepare what you will say in advance and bring all your courage and your wits because my friend, you will need them. The aim is to plant the seed, *without* putting her on the spot and making her feel awkward. … The trick is to put it out there gently, gently, without forcing her hand. That means keeping your cool and staying natural.

Once the two of you are out, get the ball rolling by talking about the stuff she absolutely loves. Bring up her background, her passions, her hobbies – anything to show you've been paying attention. Talk about the good times you've shared, the things you've done together, and the things you'd like to do again. Remind her of the brilliant night the two of you had doing such and such.

By swinging the conversation around to the personal stuff and throwing some well observed comments into the mix, you're effectively making things more intimate. If things go well, open up to her – steer the conversation towards the present moment – life in the single lane.

Tell her what you like about her, not in a creepy, awkward way, but with a light-hearted grin: *"One of the things I love best about you is that you're up for a laugh!"* Talk about your single status, obviously not in a whiney way that makes you sound desperate, but which tells her that while you're happy making the most of your single phase, you're looking forward to a relationship one of these days. Just put it out there casually. The implication is you're single, she's single. You have a lot in common and love each other's company…

By tapping into those things that she cares about, and revealing something of yourself, there's a stronger likelihood of her thinking about you within a potentially romantic scenario and then...who knows? See how she responds to the idea of the two of spending more time together doing fun stuff – without making it a big deal. You're planting a seed. Softly, softly.

Beware not to make too much a joke of it though, otherwise, she might not take you seriously at all. Tread lightly. Don't overdo it and be sincere. If you can manage a 'teaser' conversation like this, it should help you gauge whether or not she is interested. If she is, it's up to you to organise the practical scenarios to follow through and take things to the next level.

This is seriously tricky territory and sometimes there's just no explaining it. It could be that she enjoys your company and feels relaxed and comfortable around you simply because it's easy and low-threat. That doesn't mean she wants to bonk your brains out, only that she wants to be your friend. It's up to you to find out which it is because otherwise you can waste too much time in limbo-land pining tragically, and that's no fun for anyone. The trick is to stay cool and don't get too demoralised if things don't go according to plan. It's early days and there will be plenty more chances to have another pop later if things continue to develop.

And keep in mind that you're not the only one who gets trapped in the Friend Zone. It happens to girls all the time. For all you know you might have a friend who is doing, or has done her damnest to let you know she was interested in more than just coffee, but in a classic case of communication breakdown, you didn't pick up on the vibe. And she probably thought she was really obvious, but you only thought of her as a great mate. And for all the reasons we've already talked about, you have my sympathies – knowing as we do, that women can be extremely underwhelming in their attempt to let the cat out of the bag, so much so that of course you end up missing all the signals.

If that's the case, then it's likely that she gave up on the idea and she'll never know if YOU were keen on HER. How frustrating; especially if it turns out you *were*, but now it's too late!

*Last Word: If you've got a crush on a girl and want her to know you like her as more than a friend, find a way to address it without the risk element. Weigh it up first and figure out how much you value the friendship if it doesn't survive the romance assault. Ask yourself how you will cope if it all goes ape-shit. If you decide there's nothing to lose and you can live without her as a friend, by all means go for the direct approach. Do it when the moment is right and when it feels good. Otherwise sit tight and test the water without taking the risk.*

# What Women Want

Earlier on we talked about women's wish-lists, the Imaginary Clipboards in the back of our minds when we first meet you. You already know she's sizing you up based on the way you look and how you come across. But did you know she's also looking for clues about your emotional state-of-mind? Because as any woman who's been through a tumultuous relationship and the subsequent break-up from hell knows, in order to avoid going there again, she needs to be a whole lot savvier about what she's signing up for. And for that reason, women want a man who's on top of his game emotionally. But unless you're a major in Psyche, it's hard to read what's going on beneath the surface and that's why…

When she first meets you, she will weigh these things up by the way you present yourself, the things you talk about and your attitude to life. Right off the bat there are things that are important to her: She'll be listening with a keen ear when you talk about your past romances. If you constantly bitch and moan about the ex, her warning bells will go off. Likewise if you go on and on about your miserable lot in life, she'll figure you're not coping. She will pay attention to these things because she's hotwired that way. She wants to know you're stable and that you're not about to run back to your ex. Most of all she wants to know you're not a time waster, a flake or a nutter. Especially if she's been through the mill with that bad boy already!

Sharon is 32 and recently divorced. Having been through it all before, she wasn't looking for anything too complicated when she came out of hibernation to join us on a Shimmy one Friday night; she just wanted to get her flirting mojo back and maybe find a nice guy, someone she could have some fun with and over time, hopefully more. Her complaint, and it's one I hear ALL THE TIME, is that the men are vague and evasive. *No!* Obviously that's not always the a general rule, but in Sharon's case, she had the misfortune of attracting the same kind of men, emotionally unavailable men on high rotation, the dreaded commitment-phobe. Here was a woman who didn't have any problem meeting the guy or getting the guy –she just kept finding the wrong guy. Usually it was a case of meeting someone, getting along famously for few weeks until he did the Houdini disappearing act. Then he'd call three days later without a word of apology and say, *"Let's hook up"*.

All in all flaky behaviour from flaky guys which Sharon decided she no longer had time for. She wanted someone big enough and ugly enough to conduct a proper relationship. Certainly from a women's point of view, all that keeping us at a distance is baffling. Especially when all we want is to get to know you. We hadn't planned on proposing anytime soon.

So yes, I hear a lot of feedback from women who feel they're constantly let down by men, whether that's at the start of, or during a relationship. Of course they have my sympathies. But, and what I want to talk about here, is the frustration I hear from you guys, about women and why we can be so....difficult!!

And to be quite honest, we know we're no picnic. We know we come with every hang-up in the book. We know about our insecurities and monster egos and unpredictable outbursts, ready to leap up and bite you on the wotsits when you least expect it. The difference is that we're better at disguising our foibles – a face full of MAC make-up will do that!

Consider most of the single girls you're meeting today, they're likely to be fantastic girls with loads to offer, right? The reason they're still single is most likely because they lead busy, demanding lives and they've been caught up in the all-work, no-play trap. They've burst onto the single scene because one day they literally woke up, looked at their watch and went, `Bloody hell is that the time!' And with that, aged in their late twenties, thirties or even forties – off they toddled to tackle the dating arena, armed with nothing more than a Wish-List and layers of Vanilla Mist. By that time most of their friends were hooked up, so they forged new social groups.

Lovely.

But it's time consuming stuff, and when you're a woman and you've got a damn time bomb ticking away, I'm sorry, but it's stressful! So needless to say, what they found was more challenging than they anticipated. Not only do they have YOUR neuroses to deal with, they've got even more of their own. And the more you know about them, the better off everyone will be.

Milly is 32. She has a great presence and a fresh, funky look. She's blonde, petite and uncommonly pretty – a girl in ridiculous demand! At least that's what you would think to look at her. Yet she's been single since her last relationship ended several years ago. That's the reason she jumped shores and relocated to the States. But home is where the heart is, so she's since made her way back to Blighty intent on meeting a cute bottomed Englishman. Several months later, she's still not had any hits. Not one sodding hit. *What is going on guys?*

After observing Milly on our night out, I saw what was going on. It turns out that she has this idea that she mustn't flirt with anyone unless she really, really fancies them. The reason is that she doesn't want to hurt anyone's feelings. *What the…!* I'm sorry but flirting isn't just about sexual agenda! We flirt to connect. We flirt to make friends. We flirt to be social. But most of all, we flirt because it's fun. Standing on the sidelines and making conscious decisions about who you can and can't flirt with is never going to lead anywhere. It's so limiting. And it's hardly spontaneous! Especially when the choices you make are based purely on looks, and I don't know about you, but I've had chemistry with plenty of people based on something much more than what I saw at first glance. Anyway, back to Milly…

It turns out the reason she's acting this way is because she's only ever been out with one guy, and that was her college sweetheart who she married! It wasn't until a decade later when she found herself back in the dating arena that she found she literally didn't know what flirting was!

OK, great, that's the problem, but what's the solution? To begin with Milly needs to loosen up and not take it all so seriously. She needs to appreciate that flirting is fun. And that's why I sent her off on a few assignments to chat to random guys – hopefully one of them was you!

But I digress, the point about Milly and her endearing dysfunctional behaviour, is that you'd never know any of that if you were too see her sitting there, looking so perky and adorable. And when she didn't respond to your approach, you'd most likely take it to heart for all the wrong reasons. It's just another reminder that you never know what's going on under the surface. Rather than second-guess it, the best bet is to give folks the benefit of the doubt. If they don't respond because of their own neurosis, then take it on the chin and back away graciously.

Ruby is a dark horse. I first met her when she sauntered along to a Flirt Shimmy. She's a boozy, bubbly 34-year old brunette who took a while to warm up, but once her charm came hurtling through, it was blinding. On top of that she's is strikingly gorgeous, all Mediterranean complexion and big brown eyes, but she's English through and through and there's definitely a bit of the old Stiff Upper Lip going on.

But not in a bad way, she'll be the first to tell you she's made a lot of mistakes, big mistakes, with the wrong kind of guys, the result of one too many radar malfunctions. As such she's lost faith in her ability to judge. Which is a shame because she is a genuinely lovely woman looking for a lovely bloke, but, due to her past experiences she is one prickly pear and the minute anyone approaches, her guard goes up. What Ruby lacks is self-belief.

But to see her strutting around with her big sexy hair and heels, you would think she's the most confident woman on the planet. And if you were brave enough to go over and say hi and be the guy who bedazzles her, then lucky you, but so far…Ruby is only ever approached by players. And I can see why. The Ruby's of the world don't make it easy. They don't look approachable for starters, and if anything, they look like man-eaters – which can be scary, especially when the reality is nothing like that. But if you have your wits about you and you approach, you're likely to unearth a gem, a diamond in the rough. All that's required is to brave up, take a chance and go in with the best intentions.

Ruby bought along her friend Sarah, sweet, blonde Sarah, whose face dissolved into a vista of dimples whenever she smiled. We nicknamed her Smiley. But in spite of her hot, happening look, Sarah was dying inside. That's because she'd recently broken up with her boyfriend of four years. It was still raw. On top of that she found the dating scene intimidating and overwhelming. She couldn't look at anyone let alone talk to them. The idea of flirting was like a foreign language and she just didn't get it. But, since she won't be wearing a *"Nobody Loves Me"* t-shirt when you meet her, you're not to know that. You take her at face value. She looks all smiley and friendly so you assume she is. Why wouldn't you?

On that basis you approach, but you flail and flounder and finally, you tank. But since you don't know what's going on with her, or that she's dying inside, you think *you're* the problem. And sure enough, a long time after you've approached, unsuccessfully, when drinks have been drunk, the Sarahs of the world loosen up and have some fun. After striking up a chat here and there and everywhere, and getting a few well timed compliments, Sarah starts to feel alive again. Just as you look over, she's off flirting with the best of them. When you see her in action, you just want the ground to swallow you up. Not only have you been rejected, but now you're having it rubbed in your face! But you're not to know that the only problem here was bad-timing. You went in too early and approached *before* she was ready. It's just the way it is when you're dealing with someone else's neurosis. You don't know what the freak is going on.

Sometime it's the sassy girls who say it best. Annette is a super fit 32-year-old blue-eyed blonde from South Africa.

*"Living in London, a big fast city meant that there was pressure when you met someone to go home with them, otherwise you would never see them again. There has to be instant attraction and you have to be a slut.*

*I was a snob. I was insecure and I was looking for a prince. Yet once I got on the dating treadmill, and I really went for it, the experience of all those lovely chaps made me more realistic and gave me a first hand insight into what I was willing to compromise on.*

*Through the dating I also got a taste for what I really enjoyed doing, and how a date can be complete torture or really good fun. Most importantly, since I was happy to make the first move and deal with rejection, it gave me an appreciation of how tough it is for a guy to make a move. I learnt kindness and respect. And looking at myself and all my other miserable 30-ish single girlfriends who have now hooked up in past couple of years... I know it sounds like a line – but we just hadn't met the right one!"*

### Gender Specific Bollocks

While we're on the subject, let's talk some more about insecurities for a moment. Do you think we all share the same insecurities when it comes to the big two – Sex and Rejection? Do you think it's a boy/girl thing when it comes down to the real nitty-gritty of how we think and how we feel? Or do we all deal with the same crap? My theory – and history agrees with me – is that at the end of the day we've all got the same fears and frustrations, and we're all as screwed up as each other, especially when it comes to matters of the heart. The only difference is that women have the upper hand when it comes to managing it. Indulge me here...

Since we were little girls…most women have enjoyed the emotional support that women tend to give each other, whilst men have not. Traditionally we've had years of rock-hard girly bonding where we spent hours and days and weeks in tear-soaked marathons where we pored over every excruciating detail of our boy problems. As we shed our teens and morphed into womanhood, the talk-fests which were now drenched in vodka, became a big part of our lives. This was our comfort food, and as it turned out, it was much more. It gave us the basis upon which we would secure our sexual footing and cope with the craziness that we invariably went through in adolescence. This was our Boy Education where we did a double major in English Boys and we learnt it very well thank you! So of course we're ahead in the Emotional IQ stakes! That's not to say you can't catch up. Of course you can. Take a tip from *Hollywood actor* Bob Hoskins:

*"I'm a feminist, yes! Very strongly. I learned to act watching women. I read Stanislavski, and that seemed a bit obvious. I started looking at the blokes around me, and I realised that men are emotionally crippled. They've got no language for emotion, but women have. Women have extraordinary clarity. So I thought: if I can get the emotional clarity of*

*women, looking like I do, that might be interesting to watch. I've watched women ever since, I've been a stalker all my life. "* [4]

Today there are, quite thankfully, a growing army of modern men who are comfortable with their girly side and prepared to unleash it whenever necessary. Of course not all men are about the snuggly-wuggly, touchy-feely stuff, but, more and more men are starting to bandy around words like "bonding" and "meaningful" in their general day-to-day chit-chat. To be fair, it's an area that hadn't been very well served until the past decade or so, when a glut of magazines and specialist books came through. As a result a greater portion of modern men are getting used to the idea of emotional support via self-development. But generally speaking, it's a rare and lucky guy that has accessed that level of emotional IQ growing up, or has that emotional connection with his mates.

Oh sure, you go through your occasional angst-inducing phases and no doubt you've opened up to a friend over certain issues. And perhaps it's no longer true to say that most blokes would rather have a relationship with a stale bottle of ale, than talk about all this, you know, emotional shite, especially to other blokes. There seems to be a collective male hunger to get into the female psyche and understand what's going on. Hurrah! Of course you will never have the emotional experience that comes from being a woman, but neither will we have the experience of being a man, so we can't expect to get inside each other's heads, but we can try.

---

[4] *Observer Magazine 19/09/2010*

## New Kid On The Kop

Now that we've considered the emotional obstacles that are likely to appear on your horizon, think about what has held you back, and how far you are prepared to go in getting on top of it. What are the challenges you are yet to overcome?

1. What will it take to strengthen your Personal Profile?

   I need to work on getting my confidence back.

2. Describe your main potential:

   I'm smart and funny, and someone once told me I was cute (does it matter if it was my mum?)

3. How would your mates describe you?

   My mates think I'm reliable, dependable and a good bloke to have around.

4. How would you like to be described?

   As sexy of course!

### To summarise let's look at the Key Points

➤ Concentrate on getting your 'inner-self' into shape

➤ Quit the blame game – negative energy doesn't help!

➤ Tighten up your ethics radar – two wrongs don't make a right

➤ Hard-wire your PMA (positive mental attitude) into your DNA

### In a nutshell?

If you did the exercises diligently, you should find that they've opened up a can of worms. Now you need to confront them and deal with them. Think about what unnerves you the most when it comes to all this. What techniques can you use to be the superhero you know you can be?

### KPIs – *Assess your progress*

✓ *Have you got your emotional admin sorted? (Y/N)*

✓ *Are you getting rid of the baggage? (Y/N)*

✓ *Are you confident about the 'package' you're putting out there? (Y/N)*

✓ *Are you thinking beyond your type and open to any experiences? (Y/N)*

### Challenges

✓ Work on your confidence and self-esteem

✓ Focus on the 'package' and what you've got to offer

✓ Suss out any problematic 'Friend' situations

*Mantra: Rejection hurts. But it hurts less each time!*

*Written Work*

# What's holding you back in your love life right now?

e.g. Lack of confidence and fear. I'm not sure that I could handle rejection without having a complete meltdown.

# What do you hope to achieve with a strong new mindset?

To be clear about where I'm headed & less worried about what others think.

# Are you clear about what you are looking for?

I thought I was at one stage, but not now, my head's all over the place. A few bad experiences have sent me back to my shell so I need to build up my confidence and then I'll be clearer about what I'm looking for.

# What do you need to let go of the past?

I need to grow up & get out of my 'teen' mind-set!

# Q & A

*I don't spend a lot of time thinking about baggage and past relationships, and I'm worried that if I do, it's going to bring back all the bad feelings. Surely if it's not broke, why fix it?*

I appreciate the sentiment, but while it might seem irrelevant now, that thing that has been troubling you beneath the surface, whatever it is, could come back and bite you on the bum when you find yourself veering back towards a relationship. If that happens, it's likely to sabotage a new romance. That's why it's worth making the effort now – when it doesn't count.

*I don't like to think that any woman is out of my league – but realistically, I suspect that this is the case. Is there any point on making a move if that's the case?*

Yes absolutely. It's like I've said all along, you can't second guess someone's taste. Why not give her the benefit of the doubt and go for it?! Of course you need confidence to do this, but so long as you're clear about what you've got to offer, you're not going to shame anyone by having a go. People like the strangest things. That could include you ☺

*Should I go out with someone if I'm still in love with my ex girlfriend?*

It depends doesn't it? If you want to get someone out of your system, this is usually the fastest way to do it. So long as you don't break any hearts in the process. But let me ask you this, if you do hook up with someone new, will you let her know that the ex is still lurking in the background? Because it would be dishonest not to. And maybe you've got a good moral code, in which case you wouldn't dream of going there, but I'm bringing it up just in case. If it's just a fling and everyone's upfront about where they stand, then fine, go forth and enjoy it. But don't be half-arsed about it and do it for the right reasons. Don't do it just to get back at the ex.

*I know someone who's up for being a Friend With Benefits. Is there a downside to this?*

The downside is that someone will get hurt unless everyone's clear about things upfront. I think it's a myth that FWB come with 'no strings', because what can happen, and what does happen, is that one person develops feelings, and someone ends up getting hurt. Sure it seems like a great idea having that access to unlimited regular sex, and that exciting booty call – as long as no-one's kidding themselves. That means you need to be completely upfront at the outset. So long as you approach it honestly, it could be a bit of harmless fun.

*Will quiet, bookish, pro-feminist men always lose out to the laddish 'cheeky charmers', or do we stand a chance of being noticed?*

Absolutely. Yes, yes and yes! If you are smart about it and go to the right paces to find the right kind of woman that is. That means looking in the kind of places that someone discerning like her would spend time and not wasting your time trawling the singles dives!

# Step 5. Preparing For Lift-Off

# Action Man

Women are attracted to guys who lead full and interesting lives, so it makes sense that if you make your life more interesting, then others will be attracted to the new improved you, and find you more sexually tempting. True story! So, time to shun the traditional beer and pizza method of getting out of the doldrums, and do something fun instead. And since last time I checked there was no Fun Tax to pay on having a good time, no VAT and no card charges – what are you waiting for?

Recently I met up with my thirty-something girlfriend Ginni. She'd been single for so long her friends renamed her Like A Virgin! – not her fault mind because she is blonde, leggy and hot – sizzling in fact. Anyway she met this guy and by the way she talked about him, it was clear she was absolutely mad about. *"What's his secret?"* I demanded to know, aware that he had succeeded where so very many failed before him. *"He's the most exciting, adventurous guy I've ever met."* She said *"On our first date we went hiking and skinny dipped and drank wine on the beach...."*

You get the picture.

In order to be the man that Every Woman Wants, you need to step out of your comfort zone and grab life by the neck. You need to reenergise, revamp and be rearing to go. We don't want to hear that your internet connection broke so you decided to leave the house – what a turn off! Replace your habit of online porn, belching and farting with something new and lady friendly. Channel Tom Cruise's character in *Risky Business,* crank up the stereo, rock an Air Guitar and get ready to get out there. In other words, party hard or go home!

Of course it makes sense that the more active your social life and the wider your passions, the better off you will be – if for no other reason than it makes for crackling conversation. It's all about getting out there in the thick of it. The choices are endless once you get going. You're only limited by your own imagination. The more exotic and broad your interests, the more you have up your sleeve and the more self-assured you will be. So if you're determined to have a bucket of ice-breakers at the ready, and all that great stuff to talk about, you'll need a lot going on in your life. It's not rocket science, but it does require action. The challenge is to cram your Bloke's World of How Things Work calendar with fun stuff, the kinds of things that attract likeminded people. Place yourself in loads of different social environments to open up all the options. We're talking about doing anything that gets you off your backside and out there, and not just the odd football match!

Your social life shouldn't suffer during your single phase, quite the contrary – there's plenty of time for that later. There is no better time than now to indulge in your favourite things. Lord knows there won't be time when you're bogged down by the big 3: Marriage, Mortgage and the Missus! It's only once you join the couple brigade you'll realise how dull life can get, then you'll want for nothing more than to look back at all the madcap stuff you did while you were was single. You'll be the one who went out and did things and down the track you'll have so many wicked skills: comedy, cooking, cocktail-making, blah blah blah, all that fun stuff which those who have been busy with Boyfriend Duty for donkeys years, can only dream about.

The trick is to kick the habit of saying *'woulda, shoulda coulda!'* and actually do it! Give yourself the respect you deserve and book in for that something you've always wanted to do but never had the nerve. Start with baby steps to find your own personal adrenalin thrill. You've heard of a Bucket List right, all those things you want to do before you die? Well get to it. Make a list of all those things you want to do, and get cracking.

Women love to hear about the plans of a pro-active guy, whatever you aspire to. There aren't many who won't ooh and aah over a ripped Martial Arts expert, or a man who can whip up a tasty supper. Likewise a guy who enjoys fine food and company and isn't too shabby when it comes to good manners will go down a treat. As will a man who can serenade us with a guitar, piano or a poem. Aw! And if you want to get your best batting arm swinging, they say that now is the time – cricket is hot right now, a real winner with women, thanks to a certain Ms Hurley. And once you've got a bat in your hand and you're whacking that ball around, watch as all your troubles fade away.

Think of the things you've always hankered to experiment with, whether that's hopping into a stupendously sexy car and driving off into the sunset, drinking Sake, or sampling every kind of cuisine from Arabian to Zambian. Step out to the kind of places where there's plenty of cool stuff going on, from pool to ping-pong to punk-rock-karaoke. And when you're out and about – do stuff – rather than just sitting around supping pints. You're more likely to hook up with people if you're MC'ing the juke box, chatting around the pool table or belting out cheesy rock classics. That's what's great about men, they do stuff.

I'm not saying you have to become a member of the SAS or a professional Gladiator, but having an Action Man personality transplant does require a lot of doing. It's a statement that says, *'Look, I'm cool – not some boring guy living under a rock.'* But it requires more than passion; you need to plan, prepare and psyche up. Whatever it's fine food, fishing or fetish clubs that takes your fancy, you've got to get onto it. As well as doing the thing you love, you'll be meeting like-minded friends. Two for the price of one!

The direct translation is that you will have dozens of different and juicy, conversational gambits at the ready. Any man who can casually mention his DJing ability, the instrument he plays, or that he's just taken up Jujitsu is going to get a good response. Equally a man who tells us about his pursuits in higher education, his pro-level chess prowess and his ability to make clever apps, will get more than a glimmer of interest.

Fun fact: You're more likely to meet someone amazing when you're out and about doing your own thing, than when you're hunched over your PC surfing www.benaughty.com!

The pay-off is that by putting yourself out there, you will be better placed to make new friends. Not that there's any guarantee they'll be single, but that's not the point. Even if they're not single, you don't know that they don't have a hot friend, cousin or sister just waiting to quickstep out of the shadows and ravish you. Hey, it happens! Bottom line: expand your friend-set. It really is that simple!

At the end of the day, it's your life and you only get one shot at it. Spice up your life and focus it firmly around the good times. The more you put off now, the less chance of cramming at a later date. This is the time to put your charm offensive into effect. It's the man who puts it on the line and makes the effort that gets the girl. It's called greasing the wheels. Moreover know that if you don't, you'll never meet anybody new! And that won't cut it. So don't say you'll *think about it*. Just do it! Keep reminding yourself that life runs a lot better when you're in top gear. Give it your best shot so you don't look back in ten years and see that you've been walking through life on fast-forward.

Of course circumstances can impinge and make it tricky to meet new people. Whether that's because your social groups have dissolved, or your best mates have leapt ahead in the romance stakes and they're sitting pretty – all cosy and loved up, it can leave you at a loose end. But rather than moan about it, it's better to broaden your perspective and venture outside the obvious in your bid to make new friends, get out more and eventually, reach Planet Woman.

Likewise if it strikes you that your search for the perfect woman has become a little anxious – then you know it's time to shift your focus. Relax for a minute and take your eye off the big prize. Forget about looking so damn hard for the appropriate soul-mate and instead just do the stuff you love, and you might end up waking up with one.

So rather than going out with the sole intention to "pull", which can put too much pressure on the situation, concentrate instead on exploring your city and finding cool settings and backdrops in which you'll feel inspired. The trick is to think of these opportunities as practice grounds, not hunting grounds. You're out to have a good time and road-test your new skills on real life people – and maybe along the way, you'll stumble across that red hot tamale! Do everything you need to source your brand of fun.

Once you put your mind to it, you'll find opportunities galore. In the meanwhile, you will find your work productively improves, your social life rocks, and you get to do the things you've always wanted to do, which is brilliant when it comes to conversational fodder. And considering that some of the most romantic *'How did you meet?'* stories on the planet have happened randomly, you need to think outside the square. The new rule is not to knock back any invites, no matter how random they seem. There's no excuse not to do it if it's going to add a new dimension to your life. Make a pact that as of now, your answer to every invitation will be a resounding, *'Yess!'*

Banish the notion that it's easier to say 'no' than 'go' and go anywhere and everywhere – regardless of its totty potential. It doesn't matter if you're walking, talking, boozing, schmoozing or cruising. Do it because it's fun. Do it because you can. Do it because life's too short to sit on the sofa – and because the truth is – you never know where, when or how you will meet this awe inspiring woman – that's the beauty of it. It could be while you're out buying food, riding the tube, playing darts or walking in the park. You can meet her while she's in her car, at the bar, walking her dog or having a jog.

## *Are You Singlehandedly Keeping The Rock'n' Roll Dream Alive?*

You may not think a trip to the museum, movies or a live music gig will help in the romance stakes, on the basis you'll never meet anyone while you're fumbling around a dark and dusty auditorium, but you never know who's around that corner; and you could be in for the surprise of your life. I know I was when I rocked up to see my favourite band, and I met my guy.

The moral of the story is Girl Wonder always turns up when you least expect her, it may be a cliché, but it's true, all you have to do is widen your horizons – and she will come. The broader your interests, the better, so high on your list should be a commitment to honouring your heroes.

If you're a Brit Pop boy, get in touch with your Inner Rock God and make that pilgrimage to visit the homeland of your musical heroes. And don't stop there. If any of your idols are in town for a gig, book signing or performance you should be right there in the front row. Don't be afraid to pop along solo either. Why wait so long for friends to make up their mind that the chance is lost? Don't be feeling like Noddy No Mates because actually, you'll end up meeting more people this way – and who knows, you may chance upon a sexy chanteuse while you're there. In which case you'll just reach into your grab-bag of ice-breakers and the rest is dead easy.

Stop and think about what you're doing during your busy week that makes you interesting, and do those interests make potentially good ice-breakers? Are you going about your daily business of saving kittens, fighting crime and fire-fighting on the side? Or can you casually let slip that you've swum the English Channel, competed in an Iron Man triathlon, or tricycled to Belgium?

No? I didn't think so!

That's because traditionally, we're not a nation of outdoorsy types. In fact, according to surveys carried out in 2011, Britain is a nation of telly addicts with more people watching TV now than ever before. Moreover, half the men surveyed admitted they spent most of their time on the sofa. That's terrible!! Fair enough, there will be some days when you don't fancy being Action Man – those days where it feels nigh impossible to get out of the zombie-zone, when you want nothing more than to be a sofa slob and laze about with a microwave meal – does that make Brits a lazy bunch of junk food loving sofa slobs? Not according to online research by www.beriskyinpublic.com which revealed that alfresco sex survival techniques are more popular than ever! Not everyone's staying in then!

### Just The Tonic

Speaking of frisky outdoor fun, when was the last time you roughed it in the great outdoors, or, even better, at a big old dirty music festival? If that doesn't get you out of your comfort zone, nothing will! While festivals aren't official sex events, it's that heady concoction of booze, music, and the thought of outdoor canoodling, that makes them an obvious place to mingle with all the other singles, or in your own lingo, go on the pull. It's funny too, how it's essentially the same people that refuse to make eye-contact in the big cities who couldn't be friendlier at festivals. Something to do with getting absolutely spangled I suspect!

Festivals make the world go around and in terms of pulling – it's so easy – especially when there's camping involved, if you can stomach the manky germs that is! You both like the same music and shimmy your shoulders together; you drink, get smashed, have a cheeky snog and then it's just a matter of time before one of you says: *"Your tent or mine?"* It's trickier with those festivals that don't offer camping, what will you say then? *'Your portaloo or mine?'*

### Flirty not Dirty Festival Survival Kit:

*Hip Flask*

*Bubble blowing liquid (for no other reason than girls love bubbles)*

*Boxes and boxes and boxes of Wet Wipes (and Condoms)*

### *Volunteer Work*

Women love a man who does something worthwhile. Whether you work with small children or animals or volunteer in any capacity at all you'll get brownie points It doesn't matter if you're organising events or answering phones, so long as it shows your touchy-feely side. Likewise registering with Crisis or a similar charity organisation will find you in good company and offer the unexpected. I've singled out Crisis because they attract thousands of volunteers, many of them young single people. At the year's end, after the big Christmas day rush, they put on a massive party for the volunteers which has been described as the 'Biggest Singles Party in the UK'. The beauty is that you've already got an 'in' with everybody since they've all been involved at some point. The fact that they all wear name badges makes it a no-brainer. Besides all that, you'll be doing a good deed.

***True Story:*** *As we speak I find myself midway through the process of applying for a role within the Met Volunteer Programme as a Police Officer. I'm doing it so I can tell people I'm training to be a cop. Yes I am that shallow. But hey, it's a brilliant conversation piece!*

As Einstein said, *'Imagination is more important than knowledge.'*

## What's at the top of your Bucket Wish List?

1......................................................................................

2......................................................................................

3......................................................................................

# And Your Speciality Is….

It's no good having talent if you don't know what to do with it! Stretch your imagination and think about what new skill you'd like to develop and you might find you have a whole lot of fun learning, plus with the added bonus that it will give you an added boost of mystery, depth and intrigue. You'll be the one who gets out there and actually does it, while everyone else just sits around talking about it. Create something artistic that's truly and originally yours. Make your own T-shirt slogan or anything at all. Play poker and learn the art of amateur psychology for no other reason than it's useful knowing how to read people, or pick someone's mood by the way they hold their drink. No really!

Sign up to do something creative with other likeminded people – and women! Baking classes is an obvious one. Women go nuts over a man who can cook, or at the very least tries! Nail the art of making something you will be proud of, whether it's seafood bouillabaisse, sushi, Swedish meatballs or just a curry in a hurry. Explore your knowledge of thrill factor food and marvel at the bravery (or stupidity) of those who actually pay great wads of money to eat things like the deadly poisonous Japanese Blowfish. Weird!

You're probably already a barstool junkie, so why not go the whole hog and sign up for cocktail classes? Do your Masters in mixology and create your own signature cocktail – sure to be a hit with the ladies! Swill great vats of wine in the name of being a connoisseur. Throw a cocktail party and garnish with delicious, edible things grown from your own garden. And then, toast your glasses: *'Salute!'*

Make a habit of treating yourself as well. Happiness is gluttony, so become a gourmet guru and showcase your knowledge, or just do the Mashed Potato at Gastronomic Trivia nights. Get suited and booted and book yourself and a lady friend in for a swanky soiree with cocktails and canapés somewhere fab. Banish the thought that eating is cheating!

### *Get in Touch With Your Inner Kid*

Spend less time on Quantum physics and more time as a roller coaster test-pilot. Tap into your inner teen, release the thrill seeker within and get your adrenalin pumping. Relive that juvenile-delinquent angst all over again and pinpoint that moment in your life when you were infallible, untouchable and fearless. Do whatever it takes to get it back! Recall those things you loved doing as a kid and do them now! Don't be too cool for school, that's just boring. The point is to be as goofy as you can!

✓    *Relive your youth with nostalgic trip to Dorset, home of the Famous Five.*

✓    *Watch the genius of Sean Penn BM (before Madonna) in his best ever stoner role in Fast Times at Ridgemont High*

✓    *Try Rollerblading/Surfing/Hiking/ Climbing/Camping/Fishing/Go-Carting/Juggling/Bungee jumping/Sword fighting or Clown Porn. Just do something!*

✘    *Don't read Harry Potter on the train. Not everyone thinks it's normal for adults to read!*

✘    *Don't read 'Dating for Dummies' on the train.*

✓    *Do read this book on the train!*

### *Replace One Really Bad Habit With One Really Good One...*

Unleash your inner Tarzan and go wild on a jungle safari. No jungle handy? Never mind, a zoo or National Park will do the trick. It doesn't matter where you are, so long as you're out amongst nature and enjoying a different landscape. A yearning for lost Englishness can result in all sorts of adventures. Get your skates on and do something, anything. Become a self-appointed ambassador for your cause and the environment. Roam around in the country air and do your best Sir David Attenborough impersonation. Adopt an orang-utan or a panda, a labra-doodle – any animal at all. Get in touch with your inner nature lover. Do a good deed for the environment, plant a tree, grow a vegetable patch, or save an orphaned donkey!

✘  Replace sofa slobbing with

✓  *Jousting and sword fighting – a great way to stay fit*

✘  Replace Reality TV with

✓  *Beachside Boot-Camp*

✘  Replace watching reruns of *Dr. Who* with

✓  *Brazilian dance lessons*

✘  Replace buying gifts and getting ripped off with

*Making personalised arty-farty gifts with your own hands*

✘  Replace cosy weekends with smug married couples with

✓  *A visit to Nude Fest Cornwall*

## Break It Down

It all begins with your social life. If you and I were to have a little face-to-face chat; would you smile and nod and tell me that it's all fine and dandy. But then, if we looked a little closer at it, what would we see?

Let's break it down: if Friday and Saturday are reserved for friends, what are you doing with Wednesday and Thursday nights? Thursday is the new Friday after all! Are you using your free time to its best advantage? Or do you just go with the flow, in other words – the low effort options? Because if you are like so many other single blokes out there, you're probably quite happy to spend your free time doing the same thing week in, week out – hmm?

If so, it's highly unlikely that you're meeting many new people outside of your immediate group. That goes especially for romantic prospects. A reason for this could be that you're in the grips of 'incest-itis'; more commonly known as a lame approach to dating. This is a world where it's easier to hit on someone from within your group, or at the workplace, because it's less threatening, and it's the only choice on the menu. Or so you think, but I'd like to challenge that.

There's a great big world of adventure waiting out there and once you access it you won't look back, so sort yourself out and stop being an armchair fan! Book your Boys Own Adventure Weekend and do whatever it takes to get out the front door. Once you find your thing go for it. What's the worst thing that can happen? You make a new friend?

➤ **Do This:** Register at the social network www.meetup.com.

*A fantastic resource with literally hundreds of individual groups hosting events, parties and excursions – everything you can think of from galleries/exhibitions/fashion-launches/film premiers – you name it. There's nothing that someone hasn't thought of to get like-minded people along.*

231

### What To Do Tonight?

- ➢ If you're in London a quick scour through *Time Out* magazine will reveal everything going on

- ➢ Do a comprehensive Google search and scour your local papers and notice boards

- ➢ Post a Facebook message asking for recommendations

### Ticks Every Box

- ✓ *Get your social life into shape*

- ✓ *Quit the repetitious stuff*

- ✓ *Stop making the same social mistakes*

- ✓ *Tighten up your schedule*

- ✓ *Maximise every free hour!*

### Roll Up, Roll Up: What's Your Party Trick?

- ✓ ***Do you*** *have an eclectic bag of party tricks ready to entertain the troops?*

- ✓ ***Can you*** *swallow fire, and make midgets disappear?*

- ✓ ***Have you*** *had a recent stint as an adult movie star? Kidding!*

### *What are your top 5 Guilty Pleasures?*

✓ ................................................................

✓ ................................................................

✓ ................................................................

✓ ................................................................

✓ ................................................................

*Try This:* Make this your year to explore your city as though you are a tourist overseas. Get to know your home city intimately!

## Bachelor Pad

In order to hotwire your life, not to mention your love life you need to be on top of things. And since an Englishman's home is his castle, or in this case, his Bachelor Pad, that's where it starts. So gents, prepare your stations!

The modern guy is gadget-crazy and house proud – as I'm sure you are. Of course you aspire to a fabulous apartment with all the gizmos, why shouldn't you? It's a boy thing! Farewell those days of mucky laundry, bucket bongs and empty pizza boxes. An uncluttered living space equals an uncluttered mind. Slovenly bachelors be gone!

Your place of abode should be ready to rock, or at the very least, to entertain, at a moment's notice – all the more so if you are stepping out on a date and there is even a remote chance that you will bring someone back. And don't panic, we're not talking *To The Manor Born,* we're simply suggesting that your living space is organised and ready for action.

Create a calm, clean pad from which you can plot, plan and scheme your way to 007 style seduction. Don't be put off by thinking that you will lose a weekend of your life, or any party time at all, because provided you plan, you won't. Just put aside up to thirty minutes every few days for a week or two, and attack one section at a time. It's more manageable, less frustrating, and you will see the rewards of your efforts as you zoom-zoom from room to room. Take advantage of those days when you can't face the world – stay in and organise instead! It may not seem very Bond-like at the time, but you'll love the results, especially when you get to swan around like the proverbial King of the Castle.

First stop, the kitchen

A good host will have a stash of tasty snacks and drinks to hand. A choice of decent red and white wine and a spirit option will see you groove casually from coffee to Chateau le blanc and onto cocktails. If you are going

234

to invite us in for 'coffee', is it really too much to ask that it's filtered, percolated, or at the very least from one of those individual espresso bags? We won't appreciate the instant stuff when you've made such a fuss about getting us around for a coffee thanks! In terms of your cooking skills, why not attempt to perfect at least one dish so that if some lucky lady does pop over for an impromptu supper, you can wow her – some homemade chorizo at hand would be nice, so long as it's not too spicy and garlicky. Keep the snacks nice and light, you want passion, not passing out! Avoid the stuff that screams student dive, manky dishes in the sink, food strewn over the bench tops, rubbish spewing from the bins and condoms lurking around is not a good look, but a sleek coffee maker is...

**Buy This:** *Lavazza's sleek premium coffee makers for the ultimate one-shot cup of coffee.*

It may sound cheesy in the manner of a wannabe Bond, but if you want to create a vibe, then you might as well go the whole hog and bring in the clichés as well. Rock the dim lights and low music, cushions and candles. Scatter plenty of visitor-friendly mementos from your travels and other bits and bobs. Flaunt souvenirs, heirlooms, photos and junk shop finds, anything at all to give your place character and provide the all important conversational fodder. The man who can do Show & Tell, even if it's just with the much loved *'Visit from the Goon Squad'* DVD – will always have something to chat about.

It goes without saying your bedroom should be sparkling clean and all sexed up – ready for action! Have fresh sheets and linen on the bed at all times – positive thinking never hurt anyone. And what about in-room entertainment? If you don't have a projector that descends from the ceiling so you can watch films in bed, or indeed in the bath, then at the very least have your alternative or internet entertainment system set up handy. It wouldn't hurt to have a stash of Just-In-Case bits and bobs handy either. The limited edition Will & Kate souvenir condoms are sure to amuse!

235

Once you've cleared and sorted, the next thing is to confront the admin. Yes I know it's boring, but it's damn near impossible to focus on the fun stuff when you've got an anxiety disorder about, well, everything! So hop to it. Write a list of what needs to be done and tackle it one thing at a time over the course of a few weeks. Attack the stuff that's weighing you down, rather than letting it suck up negative energy. Book yourself in for those medical and dental visits. Get on top of that pile of bills, do the washing, the filing, and ring your mum damn you! Don't yawn – this is important!

Finally, don't undo all your good work by having a mingin' toilet. Most important! Clean, clean and then, clean some more! Use industrial strength disinfectant and kill that odour dead. Do whatever it takes to lose any signs of toxic sludge. Stock up on toilet paper, soap and fresh towels. And put away the X Rated Boys Toys!

### *Notice-board*

➢ Be prepared. Always!

➢ Stock up on the Just in Case goodies: booze, candles and wine

➢ Keep the bedroom and bathroom toxic-free-zones

➢ Avoid awkward bathroom sightings; warn your flatmates if your friend is staying over!

# Gonzo Travel Adventures

The well-travelled man is pretty sexy, so whether you've been a beach bum in Barbados or drinking boutique beer in Belgium, you'll exude that infectious post-holiday vibe. This is wildly appealing to women who will happily fast-forward to a fantasy life spent roving around the world with you. The other bonus is that since you won't be single forever, you need to lock down the fantasy stuff now. Live out your globetrotting dreams while you still can.

Thanks to the internet bringing the world closer together, travelling alone doesn't have to be lonely. It's easy to organise to meet cyber friends abroad, and there are of course, loads of well thought out opportunities for singles which can be the adventure of a lifetime. Once you get the hankering to go somewhere, don't waste another minute. Book that trip and hop on that plane, train or automobile. Just go!

Go somewhere exotic and cavort with the locals at the drop of a hat. Beg, borrow or steal a video camera and make your debut feature travel documentary. Even better if you learn a few words of the local lingo, and some of the more, erm, vital phrases before you travel, rather than throwing your arms around, pointing and shouting in English. Another idea is to pick up some understanding about the local culture before you go.

There are two very good reasons to do that, firstly since locals love talking about themselves just as much as the next person. The minute you show an interest in their country, cuisine and customs and in most places, you will make a new friend and slot in just like you belong.

The second and more important reason is that there is a very good chance that you will luck out with a sizzling holiday romance, perhaps rather exotically with someone whose first language is not English. In which case learning even a smattering of the lingo will help stave off any stage-fright when it comes to approaching hot babes in their native tongue.

All well and good – except that different rules apply for dating and flirting everywhere in the world, and you will encounter specific local customs. That means you need to pay attention. Especially since courting rituals change dramatically from country to country.

We are very lucky in that courtship patterns within the Western world are relaxed and interchangeable, but that's not the case everywhere. The practice of flirting has been banned in some Asian countries with the end result that offenders, both local and international, have been jailed for inappropriate behaviour. So please, be aware that anti-flirting laws are alive and well. Ultimately it is your responsibility to be respectful of local customs and abide by the rules – or face the consequences. Familiarise yourself with the local customs before you travel, so that in the event you do find yourself having a raunchy time in a new place, you won't cause any offence. Or, worst case scenario, go to jail!

### *Flirting Tips Abroad*

*#1 Rule: When in Dubai do not have sex on the beach.*

*#2 Rule: Do not attempt to flirt with the local officials.*

### Never Say Never

> ➢ *Don't lose your confidence and chicken out when it comes to chatting up the local girls because of the language barrier.*
>
> ➢ *Sort it out before you leave home!*
>
> ➢ *Learn how to say 'cheers' in every language. Salute!*

## Long Distance Relationships

Thanks to living in the technological age travelling has another bonus, that of the LDR: Long Distance Relationship. Personally speaking, I've got friends and clients who are currently in LDRs and each of them doing very well. In fact, I've got two clients with impending weddings coming up, both the result of the LDR. Wahay!! Why is it easier today? There's a couple of reasons. Certainly our communication methods are a big one. Our ability to make instant contact via Skype, Video Call, instant message, email or text, means there is literally no excuse not to stay in regular contact. Added to that, the competitiveness of domestic and long haul travel means that bargains can be found like never before. With travel options so cheap and quality communication modes so effective – what's the problem?

I find myself encouraging the LDRs on the basis that I've been there, done that, and lived to tell the tale, complete with a Happy Ending. So there you go, I am a glowing endorsement of the LDR. And so is my good friend Sian…

*"I first met Adam in Germany. He was living in Switzerland at the time, and I was based in London. We got along really well but once I got home I wrote it off as a holiday romance. I didn't expect him to be so persistent, but he was! I got lots of calls and emails and pretty soon we were having Skype calls every other night. He came to visit me in London after a while and then I went to visit him in Switzerland. I didn't know what to expect, but we seemed to fit pretty well into each other's world. As for what the future holds, I'm not certain. I've told him I don't want to live in Switzerland, and he doesn't want to live in London, but, it turns out we both have a thing for Berlin. Plus I've been learning German over the past few years since my work has taken me there many times, so who knows. Either way, I feel really positive about it."*

*New York Calling....*

*Q. I've just started dating this girl from New York, who I really like. I'm not sure if it's a cultural thing but she's still dating other guys. It makes me really jealous to think of her sleeping with other people. I want to talk to her, but I'm scared I'll push her away.*

There are gaping differences between New York dating culture and our own, especially since we don't have one! So I'm not surprised you feel jealous. And since we don't do the New York thing of dating within a systematic society, it's hard for us to relate to. But as far as she's concerned, it's just the done thing.

But let me ask, do you know for a fact that she's sleeping with other people, or is that your imagination working overtime? You're well within your rights to raise the issue, but perhaps instead of coming across all heavy about it, use the cultural point of view to kick-start a chat rather than a confrontation.

One way of testing the waters, without going on about how squeamish it makes you, is to ask her how these things work in New York. Just tell her that it's different here. The whole rigid/exclusive/non-exclusive dating thing doesn't exist here in the UK. But if she's used to multi-dating, then she might find it strange that you're not. You need to address that, so best get it out there in the open.

Keep your options open. If you make an effort to see other women, you will be on the same playing field as her. That way your feelings towards her will have less intensity and you'll be able to adopt a more light hearted approach to the current situation, even if you can't change it, at least not in the short-term.

## From Workaholic to Weekend Warrior

Like all addictions, work has its price, so while we're reshuffling things, it pays to check that the thing that eats your brain, stresses you out and takes up most of your waking life – your career – is making you happy.

It's heartbreaking the amount of time we can spend in soul-destroying jobs. And for what? The power? The money? The CV? The defining moments of your career? None of it means anything if you're unhappy. And often that's the case if you got side-tracked along the way to your vocational wherever, and woke up to find that you'd become Frustrated Freddy the Hedge Fund guru, trapped in a freelance writer's body, if that is the case, then you've got to find a way to get out because newsflash, cash is not king!

Have a good honest look at the career you're in, and ask yourself if it's the right fit. At the end of the day, you've got to respect what you do and have a conviction in your own talents, regardless of what anyone else thinks. It really is about your take on these things. It's no good if you hate yourself for doing the thing you DO, your chosen profession. You're the one doing it, so you've got believe in it. Or change your situation. Don't let yourself waste years in a job you despise or, before you know it a decade will have flown by and you'll hate yourself.

Maybe you're content in the knowledge that you've made it professionally – well done you! But ahem, what about your personal and social lives? Surely your happiness is an insane price to pay. Besides if all your energy goes into your job, what do you have to offer outside of it? What on earth will you find to talk about?

Find your work/pleasure balance and pledge to do those things that relax and stimulate you for no other reason than they're good for a laugh. If you don't have your own treasure chest of treats to hand – sort it out! Don't let the stresses of work rob you of your personality and sense of humour. At the end of the day it doesn't matter how good you look on paper, we won't want to hang out with you if you're no fun. I've been there and I can tell you, it wasn't pretty.

**Remember the Sex And The City adage:**

**"Good on paper. Bad in Bed!"**

If you are planning a career change anytime soon and fancy yourself the S & M King, or the King of Success and Money, a 90-day plan will give you plenty of time to whack your CV into shape, register with the agencies and see what's out there. If you really want to be industrious, use your spare time to invest in a mini-course and develop a new skill-set. That way you'll always have a contingency plan and you'll never get caught short again.

---

*Campbell was the black sheep of the family. His brothers were high-octane lawyers and bankers while he was a lowly barman. But he didn't see it that way, citing the brain-power it took to memorise all the cocktail recipes. Now that's what I call healthy self-confidence!*

---

# What Women Want

While we're on the subject of work, I want to talk about how the career thing influences all things to do with life, love and ladies. That's because women are passionate about the subject. I've heard it all, from the ubiquitous: *'Men are so intimidated.'* to *'Why it's so hard to meet a good guy?'* and *'They just want bimbos!'*

Naturally I'm NOT convinced.

But since the same issues keep raising their ugly head, I felt it was my duty to burrow a little deeper. As a general rule women find the gulf between professional success and personal success a very, very wide one. Why is this so? Let's take a look...

In order to get ahead in the workplace, women need to be assertive and sassy – you might call them 'ball-breakers'. You probably don't mean it in a bad way, but what you're picking up on is that – she has testosterone, and she's not afraid to use it. For many men however, that's the ultimate turn-off. Do you see the irony here? It's the very same qualities that women use to get ahead in the workplace, that conspire to work against them when it comes to you guys. It's so unfair. *Wah!*

Hear me out when I say I share the women's point of view about what's going wrong from the guy perspective. The thing I keep hearing again and again is that men are easily intimidated, or at the very least, put off by strong, sassy, successful women – the Triple S! Often that is due in part to women's professional accomplishments.

Now you might read this and shudder to yourself and say, *"No way, that's not me. I LOVE a successful woman!!"* In which case, great! Give yourself a pat on the back. But since you're minority, I will continue. For those of you who flounder and flail when you meet a marine biologist, a lawyer or a doctor, and worry that you couldn't possibly live up to her expectations, stop and ask yourself why? What's that all about?

244

Her career choices had nothing to do with you. She simply followed her passions in the same way you followed yours, whether you're a DJ, a delivery boy or a data operator. She applied herself to a particular vocation in order to fulfil herself and be independent – and now as red-blooded woman in need of nothing more than true love – she finds herself being penalized for it. *Bah!*

Part of the benefit for women who get ahead in the workplace is that it widens their romantic choices. That's because if we're financially independent, it shifts things when it comes to relationship roles. It means we don't necessarily depend on you to be the higher earner, or the bigger, better go-getter– we're prepared to share those responsibilities. And if you're smart (which obviously you are 'cos you're reading my book) then you will see that as a massive relief. We all know what it's like to live through recessions and difficult times. We have. We are. We will again! And it's during these times that the relationship roles often reverse. *"Not a problem"* say the couple who built their foundation on equality. This is the partnership which thrives because the power-balance stays the same even when the professional see-saw effect kicks in.

If we go back in time to the traditional Adam and Eve model where men wanted a real woman and women wanted a real man, you'll see it's not so different today. The roles may have become interchangeable, but what we want isn't a million light years away from what it once was. The big difference is that we're more accepting, and expecting of our partner's feminine and masculine sides.

So, what to do?

We need to change our mindset. All of us. Men. Women. Children. Because quite simply the English landscape would be a more romantic place if women were to shed their coat-of-arms – and the haughty demeanour – before stepping out of the office. But it takes two to tango and men must strive to be strong in the face of ballsy and successful women.

You can choose to believe it or not, but in today's modern society, women do place less emphasis on their partner's money making ability. Oh sure we want someone who can provide and hopefully have the means to raise a family with us, but it's not like the old days. Fewer women fantasise about having a squillionaire screeching around in a gas-guzzling sports car. That image is tarnished now, thanks mainly to dirty little secrets of the rich and greedy (did someone say footballers?!) whose dirty laundry has been publicised from every corner of the globe and served up on the dinner table with our fish 'n' chips. It's thanks in part to those debauched and very public lives, along with the ridiculous hours that the uber successful guys are forced to work, and the fact that they don't have time to spend with their family, that's taken the gloss off.

In other words we're more aware today that being super rich breeds its own batch of troubles. And I don't know of many women who want to risk going into something, only to be a divorce stat a few years down the track. Nor do I know of any woman who want to be a single mum. It's a pretty grim thought for most women.

Today we want different things. The rewards aren't so wrapped up in the material. They're more of the feel-good variety. Once upon a time we looked to marriage to provide security and a roof over our head. The emphasis was solely on income, professional status and promotional opportunity, but it's not like the old days anymore. Today it's about compatibility and how we feel. We're more interested in whether your job makes you happy, than how much money you make. We want to 'like' you, as well as love you. We want to agree on the day to day stuff as much as the Big Picture stuff. We want you to be a hands-on husband and father, someone who can take over the domestic duties at a pinch if need be. We want to have a giggle and a gossip. And we want you to be a nice guy, someone we can trust. But it needs to be a two-way street. We don't want to be penalised for being successful or outgoing or over confident. That's all we ask…

Tina is 32. She has a successful publishing career, but she's the first to admit that she is a total failure in her personal life. Yet she's as outgoing as anyone you could hope to meet. On top of that, she has the knack of attracting guys, partly because she is so outgoing, but also because she's totally hot. She's Euro-Asian with an American accent thanks to her Hawaiian upbringing. She's slim and smiley, healthy and happy and....she's been single for six years. That's the entire time she's been in London! Why for the love of god?

Admittedly she does get approached from time-to-time but, it's only by the players. So in a bid to find herself a gem of an Englishman, Tina got out of her comfort zone and tried everything from online dating to dating events and of course, coming to see me. Why has nothing been successful? Is it her credentials I wonder? She studied at Harvard and pursued a successful career in publishing and relocated countries to further her career. Do men just look at her and fall apart?

Admittedly there have been a few false starts. There was one situation where the guy chased her down so hard and then, when she finally relented, he suddenly realised he wasn't over his ex. So he texted her and told her so. Oh please! If you're not sure about your state of mind going in, can I suggest that you let the lady know before you sleep with her, not after!!

So what about the other guys that have hit on her? Well mostly it's only the very bold, and they tend to be the players. The regular guys, *like you*, seem terrified of her. Yet if you were to approach her, you would see that she's just like a big friendly puppy! She loves talking to everybody. That's the kind of person she is.

There seems to be this idea that if someone is good-looking and ridiculously successful, then there's no way on earth they'd want to talk to you. But for Tina, that couldn't be further from the truth – she's completely over being single. She wants a lovely man and she wants him now! Where are you guys when we need you? And what is it that makes you do a double-take when you see her, and then, when you find out how amazingly fantastic she is, you do a runner. I don't get it!

You're passing up a chance with a woman who has ability to make some bloke ridiculously happy. If you can find it within yourself to be a little bolder around extraordinary women, and not let the polished exterior put you off, you'll find that underneath it all, sassy women are just like you, scared and frightened and nervous.

All I'm saying is that if you see someone like Tina, hot, happening and over there...be bold and go for it. Get over that phobia of approaching a stranger. Ask her a million questions about her life, her career, her background, her world. Show her that you admire the bullocks out of her, and that you're not scared of her! Guaranteed, she'll be putty in your hands!

## New Kid On The Kop

Write down a few words to describe your new improved lifestyle.

E.g. I'll try something new once a month and go out 2 - 3 times a week. I'm good with outdoors/sporty stuff, but I need to see more gigs & things.

Now that you are set to attract new people into your life, how will you maintain contact?

I'm putting a ban on Facebook and trying to pick up the telephone more!

What can you do right away to get more fun into your life? I just need to go out more!

How will your time-table work into your regular day to day schedule? I'll sit down and look at what's happening for the week - if I give myself an extra 20 minutes, I can make plans for doing stuff during the week nights.

What have you always wanted to do, but never got around to? Loads of things, learning an instrument is the big one...

### To summarise let's look at the Key Points

➤ Fire up your social calendar

➤ Assess your working life

➤ Step out of your comfort zone

➤ Release your Inner Kid

➤ Try something you've never tried before

*In a nutshell?* *Be outgoing. Enthusiastic. Adventurous. Be Action Man!*

### Challenges:

What do you need to do to sustain a more dynamic lifestyle that will attract new people?

✓ Sign up for a new challenge

✓ Revisit your passions

✓ Make your BWL: Bucket Wish-List

✓ Travel

### KPIs: *Assess Your Progress*

✓ Have you signed up for any new challenges? (Y/N)

✓ Have you signed up for any new Action Man pursuits? (Y/N)

✓ How many different things have you signed up for to get your adrenaline flowing?(1 to 5 or more)

✓ Have you made a bucket-list – to do before you die? (Y/N)

✓ Have you made any travel plans? (Y/N)

*Mantra: A lust for life will kamikaze your love life!*

# Q & A

*There's this girl I like and we've got loads in common like hiking and camping, but every time I suggest trekking off for a weekend, she shuns me. What am I doing wrong?*

You can slow down for starters!! How about a coffee date before you try to lure her away for the weekend! There is such a thing as easing you way into it. And I daresay your crush might be taken aback by the idea of a dirty weekend as your first date. *Hello!* You may think you're sharing an interest, but she probably thinks it might be nice to have a, you know, get-to-know-you chat over a drink first! Slow down, take it nice and easy, and see how you go.

*Is it ever acceptable to chat up a girl in the gym?*

Some girls appreciate it, and even expect it. And just as many don't. It's your job to tread lightly and judge for yourself. A good starting point is strike up a conversation – well I guess you knew that already – but just keep it light and breezy and chat about the stuff you have in common: the gym, working out, that kind of thing. Try to read her signals to see if she welcomes the interruption, or is she is deadly serious about her workout? If so, she's likely to regard the gym as her sanctuary, somewhere to get away from it all. If that's the case, you've got to back off. She might get hit on all the time, and if she finds she can't even go to the gym in peace, then of course she's going to get all stressy about it, so don't push it if she's not encouraging. But by all means go ahead and ask. You know what they say, nothing lost, nothing gained.

*My girlfriend and me are very competitive when it comes to our jobs. Is that a good or bad thing in a relationship?*

A smidgen of competitiveness is healthy in all relationships, it keeps everyone on their toes, but too much of it, and it will probably all end in tears. The question you need to ask yourself is do you feel competitive rather

251

than supportive and vice-versa? And if so: why? Competitiveness is hard enough to manage in friendships, so of course it's going to be tricky when there's romance involved. A bit of friendly rivalry is fine, but if the two of you are super competitive now, fast forward to how it's going to be, especially down the track if one of you comes unstuck in your professional life. Will the other be supportive, caring, loving and all the other basic components that relationships are built on? Or not? Maybe it's best to take a good, hard look at the situation now. Talk to your girlfriend about it, she's bound to have an opinion. Find out more about the issues that are bubbling beneath the surface and address them.

# Step 6. Now You Do It!

# Hanky-Panky Happy-Hour

You've arrived at the engine-room, the Central Nerve System, your dating Armageddon. This is where the magic happens. Now that you've got a taste for how ridiculously good life can be with a bit of effort, and you're clued up to the eyeballs with what to say, you've just got to get out there, and party like a rock star.

Your final and not so gruelling challenge is to start dating. Yes dating! Since you are no longer the world's most Unflirtable Man, you will bounce from eye-popping escapade to escapade; your mission, simply to loosen your belts, let your inhibitions go, and sample all types of lovely, different sexy women. So, what are you waiting for? If you plan on licking whipped cream off a naked tush anytime soon, you need to get your strawberries out there lad!

And why not? Look at you. You're a busy man, a man with a plan. In-between making travel plans and meeting up with friends, and learning new stuff, going to the gym, and rescuing kittens and generally being the world's most fascinating man, you don't have a lot of spare time. In fact, you're so damn busy that frankly I'm surprised you've read this far – though I certainly appreciate it!

And it's all thanks to your revamped social skills that you will find new thrills and spills to generate a dating frenzy. Likewise you will know how catch the eye of Her Royal Hotness and dazzle her blind. If you approach this right and keep your eye on the big prize, you will absolutely smash it. It goes without saying that by now you will have:

✓ *Studied the big players*
✓ *Sorted out your psycho-sexual stuff*
✓ *Got on top of your day-to-day admin*
✓ *Ditched your fears about rejection and ridicule – all the R words!*
✓ *Waved goodbye to the insecurities that were holding you back*

Right then, where were we? Ah yes dating...Dating is nerve wracking. There's no other way of putting it. Finding someone and making an approach takes a lot of nerve just as chatting them up takes confidence; making the phone call takes guts, and having a first date, well we all know that can be heaven or hell.

But, I've never understood people who didn't like the actual dating process. Provided you've got plenty to talk about, your confidence is in check and you're dishing out your best lines in a swanky bar with someone drawer-droppingly gorgeous who finds you hilarious, what's not to like?

And since you'll be right in the thick of it, you'd better like it! Trying out all the stuff we've talked about – working the room, schmoozing, boozing, charming and seducing and thriving in the knowledge that you're armed with all the right things to say and do – right when Missus-I'm-Hot-For-You appears on your radar. It doesn't get better than this!

But....first you have to meet these wondrous creatures. Once you find them, you have to wow them. Clearly you need unshakeable confidence and balls of steel to pull this off. That's the point we're at now.

This is where you mark yourself out as a hardcore flirt ninja, a seeker of true life experiences and steel yourself to approach without fear. You will no longer get laughed at for being the worst dressed man on the planet, nor will you get sand kicked in your face. Far from it, you will be the Casanova of the 21$^{st}$ Century; the James Dean of the Decade, the R-Patz of the Twilight Generation. You will style it like George Clooney and swing like Errol Flynn. Your style will scream *DON'T MESS WITH ME* and your personality will cry *COME TALK TO ME* – and they will come.

## Hit-List

But… first *dunnnnnnnn-DUN-DUN-dun…* you need to get a date. In order to get a date, you need a cunning plan. Within the world of dating, there are hundreds of ways to track down the World's Most Beyootiful women. Sometimes it's just as easy as walking into a pub and looking about and saying, in the manner of a loved-up geezer, '*Right, who's up fer it then?*' and more often, it's not!

As you bunker down and become a roller-coasting dating test-pilot, your aim is to try it all. Get ready to experiment with every possible way to meet someone new. From the coffee shop approach to chatting up babes in bars, to singles events and speed-dating and of course random old skool stuff, where you just do the things you love in real life. Hey don't knock it, that's how I met my guy remember? I just turned up at a gig and smiled. I look at him now and think he's so lucky. He's got a beautiful girlfriend. And he's got me on the side. ☺

You'll be dreaming up new openers and approaches, and ducking and diving more dating divas than you ever thought possible. You'll be out there amongst it, right in the thick of it, and too busy to waste time at the Lager Loser-Boozer, because you my friend have a mission and a purpose. Of course you do, you're handsome AND clever – you're a man with a plan!

The TCA – Tactical Combination Approach to dating will give you the best ever chance of meeting a whole lot of motherloding-lovelies. This is where you lay your foundations and go forth and unearth truckloads of girls. The only pre-requisite is to be focused and energetic. The Lifetime Achievement Pulling Award goes to the guy who's putting it out there – hey, I don't mean like that, I mean the guy who is trying!

The first step is to lock down a few outings over the coming weeks, ideally between three and six. Once you've done that, you'll be one step closer to getting a date, or even better, a billion dates. As soon as you're out and about, smiling, chatting and making eye-contact, you will find that making non-stop approaches and initiating chitchat becomes effortless, especially if you've followed the Action Man plan.

The second and third steps are to get active. By alternating your time between organised dating, and the stuff you're already doing, you will be covering all bases. It's not just what you do when you're out and about; it's what you do behind the scenes as well. A world class champion is after all someone who sweats to exhaustion, even when no one is watching.

And don't turn your nose up at the organised dating side of things. I appreciate it's not everyone's cup of tea, but, they say that sixty nine percent of all couples met through online social networking sites, and personally I know of hundreds of success stories firsthand. At this stage it's a case of suck it and see. Think quantity over quality. You're transforming into a lean, mean dating machine. *Shazam!*

***Right then, time to follow up with the following:***

➤ *Step 1. Online dating*

➤ *Step 2. Organised dating: speed-dating or any other singles event*

➤ *Step 3. Real Life Event: this can be anything at all – a party, gig or work function, so long as it offers flirting potential.*


***Confession Time:*** *It's my job to flirt. If I'm out and about and I'm not flirting then frankly, I'm not doing my job. Some days I crave flirting more than others. When that happens I abandon the library and do a spot of window shopping around the Men's Department or go to some other Y-Chromosome friendly place. The point is I put myself out there and so must you. Think about women-friendly places to visit (legitimately!) Be lateral and use your creativity to try something different: Zumba classes or rock n roll dancing, there's two ideas right off the bat. You'll find lots of women in both places. No stalkage or sex-pest behaviour thanks!*

257

## Booze, Online Dating... And Sex

It makes sense to date online, of course it does – it's absolutely brilliant! No doubt you will have heard some horror stories but don't let them faze you. They occur just as much in the real world. The trick with online dating is simply to be smart about it. And since it's a stupendously, massive beast – it needs to be approached in the right way.

The first and most important thing is to establish what you want out of it. What are you looking for? Is it for fun, a fling, or a for-keeps girl? Once you're clear about that, you need to find a website that's not going to eat your brain. And it needs to be the right fit. Likewise, you really need to know what you're doing. Otherwise, you're likely to get all tangled up in it, and waste hours and hours of precious time as you trawl through billions of profiles.

I recommend trying some of the smaller independent sites, feel free to refer to my website for specific recommendations. As a general rule though, make sure the site you choose is:

a) Manageable

b) Compatible with your tastes

c) Not so massive that it compels you to spend ALL YOUR TIME STARING AT THE KEYBOARD!

The tempting thing about it, and the reason most people find cyber dating an easy way to get back into the swing of things, is firstly, you can hide behind your PC; and secondly it eliminates the hard work – to get out there and actually meet people! That's the trap. All that time spent tapping away can limit your presence in the real world. But we can't be having that, so you must follow the guidelines: don't let it bog you down and do pledge to be smart about it. Even if your previous experience of online dating has not been great, give it another go anyway. Once you're more familiar with it you will find the quality of the experience improves dramatically. Fast forward to the thrill of hearing the *click, whirr, ding* of your inbox going into overdrive. So, no excuses!

The final thing about it is that there is of course an element of lowlife scumbaggery and trickery out there, just like there is with all things online, so caution must be taken but really, just use your common sense.

# Top 10 Online Dating Tips

**1**. *Evaluate:* If you're already signed up to a dating website, look at the responses you've received so far and make a decision about whether or not it's worth staying. Be ruthless! If you choose to stay then, fine, but since the task is to broaden your search and experiment with new dating sites, you'll need to experiment with one or two new ones as well. After a few weeks you'll get the taste for the one that's best for you.

**2**. *Profile:* Put aside some extra time at the outset to make sure you're profiling yourself in the best possible way. Keep your profile short, snappy and fun. Use humour and wit in truckloads. Don't get bogged down with information overload, there's plenty of time for that later. Do get a second opinion before posting it up, preferably from one of the women folk.

**3**. *Photo***:** Does your profile photo represent you in the best and most accurate light? It's no good using Photoshop and airbrushing your flaws out if you're only going to get rumbled when someone meets you; even worse if the photo was taken a decade ago! Nor is it much good if your profile says you're a fun loving party animal, but your mug-shot shows a sultry, sulky version of you – that's sending out the wrong message. Take care to get it right the first time, get a second opinion and hopefully you will elicit lots of interesting responses to your inbox.

**4**. *Time Management***:** Implement your best time management skills and don't let the cyber world eat up all your spare time. Put aside a couple of slots a week. Set a time limit and make your online time as productive as can be. Beyond that, step away from the keyboard!

**5**. *3-Email-Rule***:** Once you start chatting with someone and you've got chemistry, try wherever possible to suggest a meet-up after an exchange of *three emails*. The benefit of jumping on the face-to-face thing so quickly is that it saves you from time-wasters, or those who are not quite what they say. It might seem rushed at first, but once you have momentum, and messages are cramming your In-Tray, you'll be well glad of it.

*6. **Health & Safety:*** If you fill a large flask with your favourite tipple before you start tapping away, you should know that the shift key is likely to get a little impulsive and that's when things can go pear-shaped. *Don't* drink and date online. *Do* keep the beer soaked tweets and messages to an absolute minimum!

7. ***Danger Stranger:*** Don't pursue anyone if they're not responding. It's illegal. Likewise don't be bombarding anyone with poetry and love letters – that could be confused with stalkage.

**8. *Use your common sense:*** if something sounds dodgy, it probably is. Don't waste time on it.

*9. **Set a target:*** Your aim is to start communications with at least three to four women in the first few weeks. If things don't go anywhere, don't waste time on it, simply move on.

*10. **Match the lingo:*** When you respond to a profile, read it carefully and try to match the tone of language the same way you would when you write a cover letter for a job application. Address all the points and try to keep your message to roughly the same amount of words as the message you're responding to.

## Booze, Organised Dating...And Sex

Traditionally singles parties have had a pretty lousy rep; a hangover from the 'desperate and dateless' days of yore. But that's all in the past, and today they've had a facelift. Today the variations of speed dating and singles parties are modern, hip and surprisingly successful for a large number of British population, so you must try them. But what I would ask is that you try not to put too much expectation on the experience. Don't think of it as the most obvious place to meet your soul-mate, that's far too much pressure, instead, think of it this way...

Organised single events provide hands down *the* most excellent place to test-drive your new skills – your own personal practice patch. It makes perfect sense. You've got a low-risk environment where everyone gathers for the same reason. That means everyone's approachable and you have a legitimate reason to approach every woman in the room. *Huzza!*

Once you're in the right environment you're giving yourself the best chance to meet new likeminded friends and possibly more. Find the best events by doing your research and registering with a company that offer the widest choices of events in your area. Have a good look for the kind of event that takes your fancy. Most modern places are quick, clever and painless; a light-hearted, fun time in a relaxed atmosphere. Try to find one that hosts parties with different components like speed-dating and salsa sessions or ping-pong and pool within the party, that's your best bet. Otherwise try something more adventurous. The choice is stupendous once you start looking. You'll find creative events of every kind with quirky themes and names like *'Down with Dating: Speed-hating'* and *'Last Night a Speed Date Changed My Life'* as well as music based nights, quiz nights, comedy, cabaret or Cuban dancing – it's all there.

In order to be successful at these kinds of events, you need to have a plan. If you've been to one, or you've been to dozens, and walked away empty handed, put it down to experience. The good thing is, you will get better at it. The secret is in casting your net as wide as possible. Keep reminding yourself it's a numbers game, it's NOT just about meeting The One. Even if you just come away with a few new friends, you will have come out ahead.

Anyone who can work the room without fear will triumph. To get that level of confidence takes practice, and practice is what we're here for. Whatever the event is, make the most of it by networking your head off. Approach it as you would a work function, you're there to meet new people and make an impression. Work your way around the room, and chat to as many people as possible.

If you are lucky enough to meet someone special, it's very important, get their number right off the bat! These events are often very big and busy and you can't take it for granted that you'll see someone again. Don't count on the dating company to provide email addresses either; in my experience this isn't always effective. Your best bet is to secure the number up front.

Often I'm asked if it's OK to keep mingling once you've met someone you fancy. They answer is yes! Once you secure a number, give the lucky lady a peck on the cheek, tell her you'll give her a call, and off you go. There's no need to spend all night by her side. It's presumptuous for a start, and if anything it can look a bit desperate! These nights are designed to mingle. And mingle you will.

Finally, if you are lucky enough to find someone who likes you *more than you like them*, then first off, you should feel flattered and applaud her on her good taste. Then, it's just a matter of being courteous. Tell her that it was very nice to meet, but you have to go. Shake her hand and off you toddle. Just because somebody likes you, it doesn't mean you have to like them back. But, it mustn't stop you from using your manners!

# Speed-dating Solutions

If you've done speed-dating before, you will know it can be pretty hairy. If you haven't, you'll need to prepare. Best to go in armed. First things first, what to talk about? Or what not to talk about? We've already discussed deflecting the dreaded *'What do you do?'* question in favour of the fun topics – not too tricky since any topic is more fun than work! But if you find you *have* to talk about what you do, then keep it short, sharp and change the subject before it can get too involved. Hopefully your playmate will follow suit.

Grab her attention and make your opener a killer: so you swam the English Channel last year? Great. Tell her! You regularly rescue orphaned donkeys? Fab. Mention that! You wrote a comedy rap and posted it on YouTube? Throw that in as well! Just remember when you talk about your own interests to use it as a lead-in to ask about HERS.

Don't get bogged down with a fact-finding mission, steer the conversation on course for fun and focus on:

*Favourites*: Drinking places, restaurants, holiday spots and fun weekend things to see and do.

*Seasonality*: Easter/Bank Holidays/ Halloween/Guy Fawkes/Xmas/New Year/ What holidays or special events are coming up you can talk about?

*Topical:* Have some big news stories and topics up your sleeve. Are you in the midst of the earliest ever snowfall or longest summer?

*What else are you both experiencing at this time?*
*Prep:* Swot up on the latest human interest stories/celebrity goss or general global craziness. Link it to some funny, feel-good story that's making news at the moment and focus on the positive stuff.

*Try these bad-boys for size: The Whaddabout You? Questions*

- It's my first time here, I love this bar; whaddabout you?
- My drink is Redbull & Vodka; whaddabout you?
- My favourite band is Muse; whaddabout you?
- My all time fave DJ is MC Fried Brain Cells; whaddabout you?

*Always keep a stash of Who, What and Where questions:*

- Who was your idol as a kid?
- What was the first record you ever bought?
- What is the last CD you bought?
- What was the first concert you ever saw?
- Where in the world would you most like to be this weekend?

*Have plenty of random questions at the ready:*

- You can live anywhere in the world, where would it be?
- Favourite way to spend a Sunday afternoon?
- Morning or night person?
- How far would you go on a first date? *NO! Just joking, NEVER ask this question!*

*Now it's just a matter of keeping the conversation going...*

- Who in the whole world would you invite to dinner?
- If you could be someone else for a day, who would it be?
- [5]Only for the very cheeky, 'If I was coming for supper, what would we eat?'

---

[5] If you live in a one-horse town where there are no dating events you will need to hatch a plan to travel to the nearest Flirt Zones. It may be a hassle, it may be time consuming and it may be expensive, but, if you're committed to the cause, you will do whatever is necessary. No excuses!!

## Remember your ABC's

**A = Ask** the W Questions: What, Where and When

- <u>What's</u> been the highlight of your week?
- <u>What</u> do you normally do on a Saturday night when you're not in this neck of the woods?
- <u>Where</u> did you learn that?
- <u>When</u> did you do that?
- <u>What</u> are your plans for the weekend
- <u>Where</u> are you going? Come baaaack!!!

**B = Be** yourself: Your playmate will take it as a massive compliment if you say what you think. I know it's not very British and all, but would it kill you to try? Start with the easy stuff:

*You're funny!*

*You're fun!*

*You really know your music!*

*This is the most I've laughed all week!*

*I love coming here because interesting people come here (smooth!)*

**C = Collaborate**: This is a team effort, a game of give and take. Make every effort to put your playmate under the spotlight.

*Make her feel like The Only Girl in The World.*

# Real World Stuff

Once you've sampled a few speed-dating sessions and strutted your stuff online, it's time to try your luck in – the Real World, either at the new spots you've unearthed, or some of the more female-friendly spots you normally go. All the while you'll be keeping an eye open for someone with whom you can have some friendly banter. And then...*bam!*

This is the part where you make an approach on a random stranger for no other reason than *you can*. It takes guts and it takes gumption, but by now you've got that in spaces and you're totally up for it, right? And what the hell, it's the 21$^{st}$ Century; we live within the freedom of a western civilisation, so you've got nothing to lose. Am I right?

***Now that you're familiar with all the gesticular hostilities and testicular possibilities, it's time to:***

✓ *Road-test your fancy-pants new skills*

✓ *Channel all your dexterity*

✓ *Convert your energy into a truckload of heavyweight dating*

✓ *Propel your social life into the stratosphere*

# Location, Location, Location

For seduction tactics that are shaken and stirred, you need to spread the love and clearly, the more you do, and the more you partake, the better your chances will be So, where will you go to flirt? In terms of the more obvious flirt-zones, you can't go past the bar and club scene – pretty much anywhere where there's entertainment and booze. It's amazing what alcohol can do to loosen up the flirting muscle – funny that! So, while it may be wholly unoriginal, it does make sense to wade into a big old dirty pick-up joint to kick-start things. So long as you don't fall into the trap of *depending* on bars as your only source of flirting fun.

It's only when you abandon your regular posts and try somewhere new that you stumble across all sorts of opportunities. Remaining as wide-eyed as though you are a tourist on an overseas jaunt, pledge to get to know your home city more intimately. Have a cultural smackdown and embrace the massive choice of music/comedy/dance venues that we are so lucky to have at our disposal. Use your imagination to source fresh flirting hotspots. The trick is to think laterally.

Ditch those endless nights spent knocking back pints in *Ye old Fighting Cock*. Hanging around the same old boozer with the same mates every Friday night, and moaning about your lot just won't cut it. Nor will mooching around posh cliquey bars where air kisses are fired like rounds of ammo, but, no-one actually like – talks – to each other. Avoid the snooty *Club Wotever*s with their self-conscious scene; hanging around places like that won't do you any favours. Pick somewhere fabulous instead – not somewhere all fake and posy, but somewhere where *you can be fabulous.*

There are so many fantastically themed venues about, find the ones that bring out the best in you. Dress the part for a 20s theme night at a modern day speakeasy and drink lethal gin cocktails from teacups. Leap around at theme nights dressed like your favourite 80s rock star. Jump around like a twat and dance your head off. Being cool is old hat. Having fun is the new black.

Think outside the box. A fine English tradition is queuing. Queues offer more flirting opportunities than you can poke a stick at. There is nowhere better to do this than London, where most of us spend half our time in queues! Thanks to your new improved social life, you'll be rocking those queues in as you wait for bands, booze, bus tickets and more bonza stuff As for what you will say once you are in this illustrious queue, refer Ice-Breakers and Openers.

Or, do what I did. Go to an unfamiliar area, find a happening bar, and just wander in. Take a seat, preferably amongst a lively group, and busy yourself with whatever prop you've got, your newspaper or laptop, exactly like I'm doing right now.

Here's the scene: it's around 9.00pm on a summery Friday night. Rather than go home and sit at my desk and work, because the love of my life is away and it's lonely and life's too short, I've popped into this happening bar where I can perch on a table and finish my work. It's located in a secret courtyard off the main drag in Kings Cross. It's only twenty minutes walk from where I live, but I've never been there before and the crowd is an eclectic bunch – just my taste. It's a Spanish Bar with sexy beats and soft lighting giving it a fantastic atmosphere with food that smells amazing! Judging from the amount of single sex groups, it's looking like a good old Sausage Fest – with quite a few more men than women.

Right then, back to business, let's see if anyone fancies a chat. I'm looking quite industrious as I tap-tap-tap away, but I'm also doing the lighthouse: looking here, looking there; signalling that I'm approachable. Let's see how long I have to wait. It's been five minutes so far. It doesn't usually take this long. But then I am an attractive woman ☺

Ok I'm bored with waiting. I'm going to make an approach on the three guys behind me. *'Excuse me'* I say, and ask what the bar is called. It's called *Camino*. The guy who answers seems friendly enough and takes the trouble to show me the name written on the menu, but he goes right back to eating his tapas. In the manner of a typical Brit, he's not going to say a thing. If he was smart, and he wanted to chat, he'd ask me if they had Wi-Fi here.

*News-flash.* Another guy has just come over and sat on the table right by me. He's not saying a thing but he makes eye-contact. Then he gets up and stands about ten feet away, on his lonesome, glancing over at me from time to time, which I think is really strange, because he could have said anything when he was sat at the table, and I would have quite happily chatted. Anything to get out of work right? Kidding! ☺

*Breaking News:* OK, this is bizarre, and true, I should probably mention that I'm a bit tipsy now – so sue me! Anyway, this tall, blonde guy has just come up and asked, *'Excuse me, but are you a comic....did you do a gig in Crouch End last night?'* I look at him in disbelief. There's no way he could be making this up. As you know, I am a comic, yes. And I did do a gig in Crouch End last night! He goes on to tell me, that he was there. He was sitting somewhere in the middle, he said, but, he had a really big, messy night and couldn't remember much of the show. He did remember I was Australian though – ten points. Take note readers, by this time he's managed to manoeuvre a chair next to me and sit down. Not only that, he has asked what I'm working on, and I've told him, because that's the kind of girl I am. It's all market research innit?

We chat for the next ten minutes. And then, guess what he tells me? He wasn't at my gig at all! His mate, over at the bar, was at the gig with his girlfriend, and they recognised me. He took the information, repackaged it, and presented it as his own! And what did he get out of it? Oh only the perfect opener! What an opportunist. Granted it was cheeky, and it was a lie,

270

but a harmless one. It was also smart and ballsy. So there you go. I just thought I'd share that with you because as you know, I love it when a guy goes out on a limb. More importantly, I love being a recognisable comedian. *Bravo!*

The message is, don't turn your nose up at doing random stuff. This is what it means to get out of your comfort zone. Putting yourself in different situations and taking a chance can make you feel invincible; almost like you're in another city, or country. And don't confuse taking a chance with a sleazy approach – because provided you can pull it off, it's always going to be more cheeky chappy than sleazy.

***Upon Making Your Approach***

✓   *Stick to the things you would say in real life*

✓   *Tailor your opener to the setting and make it relevant*

✓   *Adhere to the KISS: Keep it Simple Stupid theory!*

✓   *Don't overcomplicate it and don't over think it*

## How's Your Approach?

Once you've researched your flirting hotspots, you'll be set to get out there and practice your social jujitsu. The idea is that by making an approach here and there, it won't seem like such a biggie. Initially all you're doing is testing the waters. You'll soon know if there's a good vibe, or any vibe at all. If not, there's no harm. The key thing is to approach cheerfully and without fear. There's no need to have a meltdown. If it all falls to bits – step away from the lady. It really is quite simple. Yet…

Don't be surprised if the old performance anxiety rears its ugly head the minute you're about to 'go in', we'll address that bugbear in more detail shortly. In the meanwhile, keep your radar finally tuned for girls who are approachable. In your heart of hearts, you know the ones who are going to turn on you with a twisted, angry pout and hurl violent abuse. Avoid her by all costs and go for the friendly ones instead.

The girl I'm talking about is *not* Miss Universe and she's *not* a plastic-fantastic wannabe who refuses to speak with any old piece of tosh, least of all one who earns less than a gazillion pound a day. The girl we're talking about is just your average cheeky chicky. She's sweet, genuine, and as cute as a button. She might not be flirting bombastically with you, but nor is she flirting with everyone else in pants. She might be shy or unsure about her sex appeal. But one thing's for sure, she's not a stuck up bee-atch!

*'Fine!'* you say, but you're still not convinced that you should put yourself out there for possible rejection – when the rationale is simple. It's not your place to second guess anyone or short-change yourself. You're becoming *liberated*, free from the chains that stop you from living – really living. Of course it's tricky to make a move if there's no Green Signal, but we've seen plenty of examples where the lack of signal, have made it impossible to gauge. So, in the spirit of taking a chance, and leaping before you look, you will need to take a deep breath and saunter over and say *"Alright gels?"*

272

### *Improve Your Exposure (don't take that literally)*

Picture the scene. There you are, all suited and booted and out with your mate. Together you're striding confidently through a dimly lit bar where the women drink Bacardi Breezers and the men buzz around them. You're in and out, light on your feet, sparking various chats here and there and everywhere. You observe the groups of party goers and then – crikey – as you're trawling the bar, you look up and there she is.

A lone and lusty lady seated by the bar. Pretty-girl, rock chick, soul diva, boyish babe, city slicker, whatever you fancy – she's it. You spot her and seconds later you've sauntered over to the bar to order a drink. She looks around, clocks you and, shock horror, she flashes you a smile. You smile back, do a polite little side-step dance, and then you look at her drink.

She's drinking champagne. Or so you think.

*'Champagne?'* you say. *'What's the occasion?'*

*'It's actually Prosecco'.* She says with a smile.

*'Ah'* You say: *'So what's better, Champagne or Prosecco?'*

And from there a ten minute debate ensues. *Bravo!* Now you've just got to find the Jackpot Moment. Keep driving the conversation until you find the natural 'close':

You say: *'Where are you from?'*

She says: *'Australia'.*

You say: *'Whereabouts?'*

She says: *'I'm based in Sydney but I grew up in Melbourne'.*

You say: *'I went to Melbourne when I visited Oz a few years ago, it was my favourite place. I LOVED it!'*

She says: *'You clearly have great taste. YOU ROCK!!'*

You say: *'I HAVE to show you the video I made. How about you come over to mine? I'll make us an Aussie-themed dinner – croc burgers, roo bangers – all the Aussie favourites…!'*

She says: *'Yes please!!'*

And by crikey, there you have it! Next thing, the two of you are chatting and laughing while she's ticking all the boxes as you:

✓   *Buy the drinks and lean in closer*

✓   *Extend your eye contact and brush her arm with every hilarious punch-line*

✓   *Ask open-ended questions and listen closely to the answers*

✓   *comment on her necklace: big shiny beautiful baubles*

The conversation flows like liquid sunshine, the only thing niggling away at you is that you chose today of all days…*to wear your large greyish underpants! AAAARGH!!*

## Closing the Deal

You move in nice and close. You've found flirty excuses to brush her arm, her shoulder, her hand... She's been all smiles while you've dished out manly displays of humour, using your clenched fist to punch the air and emphasise your points excitedly. It's all going very smoothly, she's laughing her head off, and as for you, you're on fire! You like this girl and you have a good feeling about her...especially when she says, *"What would you like talk about?"* You chuckle and say, *"Your phone number!"*

Of course it never happens like that, so you have to be poised and ready.

If you've been paying close attention and watching the signals, the body language and most especially her *eyes*, you would know if you qualify for her, *I'm Hot for You!* short-list. Come on, you should be an ace at this by now! If all the signs are there and you're feeling like the most self-assured man alive, then, ask yourself, what are you waiting for?

### *What's the best way to get her number?*

Rather than waiting until all the fun has died down, strike while the iron is hot. Don't be breaking out in a cold sweat right as you're about to ask. Likewise, don't wait until the moment is lost and then ask when everything's gone all quiet – that's just awkward. Much better to get right in there and do it while you're on a high.

Act decisively and show her you mean business. If she asks loads of animated questions in response to an interest that you've bought up, get in quick with a great big enthusiastic: *"Let's meet up later. I'll show you..."* And then, go ahead, whip out your phone and get her number before she can change her mind. Close the deal already!

You'll know when the moment's right because you'll be bonding over the same thing, whether that's your favourite film, fetish or football team, it doesn't matter, the key is to JUMP when the moment appears. Then it's the most natural thing in the word to get out your phone and go for it. You've already got a legitimate reason to say,

*"I want to try it as well! What's say we hook up and do it?"*

There. It's low-key, it's completely in keeping with the conversation and yes, it really is that easy!

Likewise, if you're secretly hoping she'll come out with you afterwards – what you could say accompanied by a big grin is:

### Case #1 *"We're hitting a club later, you'll be coming with us yeah?"*

It keeps things nice and light and breezy and there's a good chance that she'll say, *'Yes!'* Of course it's cheeky, bold and cocky, but erm, that's the point!

### Case #2: *You both wind up at the same party some time shortly after you first met, what's your strategy. Do you?*

Give her a kiss on the cheek and let your shoulder brush hers as you grin and say:

*"I hope you know I'm planning on dancing my head off tonight – with you!"*

That'll do the trick nicely thanks. It's forward, but not too OTT, and it gives you the go-ahead to stake her out on the dance floor later. *Yess!*

### Case #3 *Her friend comes over, what do you do?*

At ease soldier! This is a golden opportunity to use your charm on the friend, whilst establishing a sense of intimacy between you and the Hot Babe. The way to do that is to act like old mates. Strengthen the bond by talking to the friend about the conversations you've been having:

*"So, Sally here was just telling me about....(fill in the blank)"*

### Case #4  Uh-oh, Awkward Pause Attack!

If everything is going hunky dory and then there's an awkward pause in the conversation; throw in a curveball by asking about:

✓ Her best ever holiday
✓ Her favourite animal
✓ Her views on men waxing their privates. *Or, maybe not!*

Use the samples from above, but also, try to generate your own. The chief thing when you try the Ice-Breakers, is that you do so with a genuine smile on your face – not a fake one that fades away to reveal the world's biggest grimace!!

### Don't panic

➢ Use Ice-Breakers to get the ball rolling
➢ Use your location and props to drive the conversation
➢ Find a way to make that connection and find the Jackpot Moment.

### The Cock Block

Frankly if I was a man, I can see why it would be mildly terrifying to make a move on a gaggle of girls (a group of two or more) which is why I'm all for approaching girls who are on their own, or those in unevenly numbered groups. Three is good because you've got more chances of the other two talking amongst themselves, while you chat up the Hot Babe. What are you meant to do if you spot some cute girl out with her four besties, especially if it looks like they're not going to appreciate the interruption?

There's a couple of ways to approach this. One is to chicken out – but clearly that's not an option. The other is to square your shoulders and get in there! I realise it takes extraordinary confidence, but if you're game, it could be the best thing you ever did. Remember the story of the *Time Out* party guy I told you about at the beginning, the hero, the legend? He had the *cojones* to do it, and he never looked back.

### How long should you wait before making contact?

If you get the number on Saturday night, and you say you'll call tomorrow night, then call tomorrow night! It's pretty idiot-proof. If you don't want to call that soon, then don't. Go with a 2-day rule or a 3-day rule. It's not that complicated. You're the boss. You decide. Just call when you feel the time is right. Give her a bit of breathing space, but don't leave it so long that the memory of you fades into oblivion.

### Text or Phone?

Ringing is preferable, but there are risks, like if you ring at the bad time – you're screwed. So, rather than catching her at the wrong moment, why not text ahead and ask when is a good time to call? If she comes back with a response, you're in! If she doesn't, leave it a day or two and then take your chances and give her a call anyway.

If you get the dreaded voicemail, by all means leave a brief message but don't whatever you do go on and on. A snappy *'Just calling to see how you're doing'* will do the job. Don't ask her to call back because it's not the done thing, plus you'll have to play the dreaded waiting game which is NOT FUN. In fact, if you haven't already watched the film *Swingers* about what NOT to do, then go and watch it now!

If you want to keep it casual, opt for a breezy text message saying: *"Fancy a few drinks if you're about one night this week."* It's light. It's to the point. And, it gives her the option to choose the night she'd like to see you, rather than restricting her to the dates you've suggested.

## She's Not That Into You

Once you're ready to go out into the night and forage for fistfuls of phone numbers, pause to consider first where it could all go wrong. For the most part, women are receptive to light-hearted approaches, if for no other reason than it makes them feel sexy and popular and – it's good for their ego. Plus they get to show off in front of their friends. Once you make a triumphant approach and find yourself having a chat and a laugh, that's the moment you're both in it together, at that point, it's a team effort, without which, you're pretty much screwed.

### *What To Do If It All It Goes Twats Up?*

But, assuming it doesn't happen the way it happened in your fantasies, what's the worst upshot if you make an approach and she's an A-hole about it?

### *Scenario 1.*

You meander over with your widest grin and say *'You right!'*

She barely looks at you but swirls quickly away.

She's ignoring you big-time.

You stand there like a stunned mullet not knowing what to say.

She swivels towards you and glares at you with complete and utter disdain and just as quickly turns her back on you

*Ouch!*

Slowly and torturously you die, clenching your buttocks in embarrassment.

You glance back over your shoulder hoping to god that your mates weren't watching.

Who can blame you for feeling like shite?

Especially if she turns to her friends with a smug expression on her sour little face that says: *"Why am I the one always getting hit on?"*

How would you feel?

What would you do?

Do you take it on the chin and shrug it off because you're a big boy?

Or run away to your bedroom and slam the door and scream: *"I hate you anyway. So there!"*

Chin up. Look at it this way: if you were brave enough to go to battle in the first place and you get a kicking, you've got to take it on the chin and go down swinging.

And really, so what if things didn't go as you'd hoped? Hey-ho, shit happens.

Respect the lady's decision and move on. There's no need to over-analyse it. When all is said and done, you didn't embarrass yourself too badly, not if all you did was to make an approach and you were rebuffed. Big deal. It happens to the best of us. No doubt it's happened to the very vixen who dished it out to you. *Next!*

The key thing is don't, I repeat, DON'T freak out. We all get the heebie-jeebies, but what are you gonna' do? You've simply got to enforce a stiff upper lip, keep calm and carry on. Then it's just a case of clambering back onboard and barrelling upward for your next experience. The important thing is to pick yourself up and dust yourself down if you fail. And you will fail at some point. No one comes out of this unscathed.

This is about rolling with the punches and taking it on the chin. That's what the Pros do. You don't see them take their bat and ball and go home when they screw up. They don't get going when the going gets tough, and nor should you. Don't let this one crappy incident destroy you and don't let it affect your game. Put it down to experience and laugh about it over a pint with your mates. Celebrate it whether it's a car crash or not. Because even if you're smarting like hell, at least you know you're alive. It's like anything in life; you've got to fight to be a contender. This is only the first round clash. You're by no means outclassed and you showed guts. As awkward situations go, it's really no more terrible than any other. Worse things have happened and will happen again.

The secret is not to let the small stuff turn into a big deal, especially if you don't even know the woman well enough to care about, not in a meaningful way anyway. You mustn't give anyone the power to hurt you – she can't hurt you if you don't let her.

What matters is that you pointed, clicked and whirred and made an approach. And whether it was the nerves that malfunctioned, or that the woman was a complete and utter nightmare, it doesn't really matter. The point is you tried, and the less personally you take it, the easier it gets. Humans are hotwired to experience stress in certain situations so of course you feel unsettled! But, in order to get to the good stuff, you've got to experience the good, the bad and the ugly. Just remember – emotional detachment.

'Oh sure', you might be thinking, 'How can I not take it personally?' To which I would respond, who knows what's going on with her? You're not inside her head! It could be any number of things: maybe it's that time of the month, or she's just been dumped. Perhaps she's just come off the Prozac, or the batteries on her Roger Rabbit died and she's testy as all hell. In other words, it's not you – it really is her!

### At What Point Do You Give Up?

Let's say you've given it your best shot and nothing's happening. If anything, it's all gone a bit Pete Tong, what should you do? Throw your hands in the air on the basis that she's not keen?

No!

Not yet anyway.

If you don't know her very well, you don't know how she usually acts in these situations. It could simply be that she's shy, reserved or socially anxious. Give her the benefit of the doubt, at least for a good few minutes. If she still doesn't get it after you've kamikazed her with your charm, swerving daringly between smouldering eye-contact and shoulder grazing, while your hand brushes hers, only to find that she twists her body violently away – then you know the drill, hold your hands up in a surrender pose, deny and confirm nothing, and step S-L-O-W-L-Y away from the lady!

At this point it's fair to assume that she's just not that into you. Sorry for being harsh. I just don't want to see you waste your time and energy. If you're getting nowhere in your attempts to crack the access code, give it a rest, at least for a moment, because if you hang around for too long, and try too hard – you will come across as a pest, or worse still, desperate. The key is to listen to your gut reaction and be *honest* with yourself. You'll only get grief if you overstay your welcome, and deep down, you probably know it. But if you want to persist because, you're a man, and real men conquer treacherous terrain, then go for it. But don't come whining to me when it all ends in tears.

The first law of getting out of an awkward situation is simply to head back to base. If you really want to, you can glide by a little later and see where the land lies, but only if your flirt-uition tells you it's the right thing to do. Not because you've downed nine Jagerbombs in three and half minutes and you're primed.

282

***When in doubt, ask yourself what would George Clooney do?***

But, and I'm playing Devil's Advocate here, if you turn that situation on its head, you'll see how she could quite easily get the hump and decide *you're* not interested if you DON'T go over and say hello, or worse, if you do go over, and you make one false move, like looking over her shoulder, in the direction of another Hot Babe, as innocent as it may be, she will conclude in two seconds flat that you're not into her. You really cannot underestimate how sensitive women are!! *Oh puhlease!*

### *DUNNNNNNNN-Dun-dun-dun...*

There are vicious women out there, they do exist. I refuse to sit here and deny that, or defend them. Likewise there are some women, and I'm talking about the real Top Totty, often (but not always) the prettiest and most popular, who have been hit on so often that they've developed an aversion for it. So if she's like a bruised banana – nice on the outside, but all brown and rotten on the inside, or she's vile or rude – then you've got to be big enough to accept it gracefully – dip your cap and move on.

### *Scoreboard: One Love*

Anyway, who said all rejection was all bad?

*Cock a Snook*

*So long as you followed these rules <u>before</u> you gave up the game:*

> You waited for the right moment to corner her

> You didn't interrupt while she was pouring out her deepest darkest secrets to someone else

> You delivered your signals with clarity and purpose – not in a 'blink and you miss it' way

> You were crystal clear with the signals you were sending out and repeated them frequently

> You watched carefully for the signals you got back and responded accordingly

> You smiled a lot and said interesting things and got to ask a few questions

> You gave her a chance rather than running away with your tail between your legs

## Signs, Signs, Everywhere are Signs

DO read the signs. DON'T ignore them and don't badger someone if they're not keen. You might get them in the short term but you won't keep them. They'll always have the upper hand simply because you like them more than they like you. That will only end in tears.

***Try It! Ditch It! Switch It!*** Experiment with different techniques and be prepared to switch tactics if things don't go as planned.

***Buyer Beware:*** As an aside, I do warn the ladies about unwanted attention and I will do the same for you. We've all been the subject of it at some point and like I said earlier, there's only one way to deal with it: use courtesy, manners and diplomacy. There's no need to be rude or obnoxious, just be firm. A simple: *"It's been nice chatting, but I have to say goodbye"* accompanied by a handshake should suffice nicely.

Likewise if you've morphed into that arrogant, obnoxious guy we've all had the dreariness of dealing with; or you're leaping over her like a drunk, lecherous glob, pitching out lines like: *"I think you should know, my specialty is sexual harassment."* Know that she will not hesitate to use the emergency exit hatch, or call security!

***Spot the Difference....*** How do you know if she's into you? If she says: *"Look Barry, Garry, Larry whatever your name is, thanks for making the effort, but Goodbye!"*

You know the drill, step away from the lady!! Which brings us to…

***If you're in a hole stop digging:*** In order to make progress you need to feel the pain. Going out on a limb lifts the spirit, just as rejection annihilates it, but only if you let it. You will crash and burn along the way – all the best flirts do but if you just keep on trucking with a smile on your face, you'll go along way. You're a trooper; and a contender for the Bravery Awards. Well done you!

***Judges Verdict:*** *Keep things in perspective. Sticks and stones may break your bones, but turds can never hurt you.*

***Fizz. Bang. Wallop.*** *If you don't take risks, you'll never get to experience anything exciting.*

***It's Not Fair:*** You see a woman wearing a T-Shirt with, *"I ♥ cute guys"* sprawled across her chest.

You wander over to introduce yourself.

Your advance is met with "Get lost Bozo!"

What can you do? Whinge? Moan? Complain?

No! Go and try again with someone else!

***Word of Warning:*** Don't go overboard. You'll only come across as intense which can be scary. Nobody wants to hang out with a psycho-stalker!

### Kiss Me Quick!
Assuming things do go well, there will be some other tactical situations to consider, like… when she cocks her head towards you, is that a clear and direct sign to kiss her? Or is it just because she is a whole lot shorter than you? Should you risk it, or err on the side of caution? And is it OK to kiss her on the first meeting? Of course there are no sure-fire answers to these maddening questions, all you can do is follow your instincts, trust your judgement, and suck it and see!

### Don't Be Getting Stonkered
*If you're tempted to down three pints to get you warmed up before you've even made a move –can I just day don't! You'll be blowing warm beer in her face and making a face that says: "I'mshnotasdwunkasIseemhic-really! And the thing about that, is she won't understand a word you're saying!*

286

***Final Word:*** If you do manage to get her number, don't be a Muppet about it – call her! Good golly gosh, that's why she gave it to you. At the end of the day women just want a man who calls when he says he'll call!

# Q & A

*I had a date a week ago with a woman who I thought was great. The chemistry was there, we were sparking off each other, but when I texted her to ask for a second date, she blew me off – what could I have done differently?*

Would it not have been better to ring since it was a second date? You've already crashed through the barrier with Date No. 1 surely the goal is to become more personal, not less! Plus it's harder to say 'no' to a human voice. Never mind. It's nothing that a simple case of persistence – by which I don't mean stalking – will recover. It's perfectly reasonable to go in for a second round; there's no reason not to. You might have caught her at a tricky moment when she was genuinely too busy. Try not to be put off and don't lose your nerve. Give her a couple of days and then, get on the blower. Psyche yourself up, use your most self-assured voice, and dazzle her by suggesting an outing, someplace that you know for certain, she will love! Good luck with it!

*I recently bumped into a mate's ex. I'd always fancied her and I had an inkling she liked me. We ended up having a drink and one thing had led to another. I felt horrible afterwards and I think she was weirded out as well. What happens now, do I tell my mate?*

I think we all know there's an unspoken rule with this kind of thing, but you chose to go there, so you have to deal with the consequences. No matter why they broke up, or who broke it off – there's not many souls who would like their mate 'going there' afterwards.

Let's look at two likely scenarios: firstly, if you don't tell your mate, he's likely to find out anyway. Secondly, you've got to consider the possibility that it may have been a 'revenge shag' (sorry to burst your bubble). If so, the ex will no doubt gloat about it, to your mate, in which case he will be down on you like a ton of bricks for not coming clean. If you tell him before he finds out, and that would be the decent thing to do, you

288

should be prepared to cop it sweet. This is not going to be your dirty little secret for very long. You weren't thinking about his feelings at the time of the indiscretion, now it's time to face the music.

### What if my mate likes her, but it's her and I who have the chemistry?

Mates don't steal girls from under their mate's nose, not real mates anyway. If your mate is stuck on her and he saw her first, then, don't mess with it. Leave him to it. There's a lot of fish in the sea and life's too short to create a rift with a mate over a girl, isn't it? Anyway, if it is what you think it is, she'll find a way to let you know. That way if something does happen, you can hold your hands up and say: *"It wasn't me, it was her!"*

### I've just started to see this girl who I really like, but she texts and calls me all the time and it's putting me off. How can I tell her to back off?

Human psychology determines that everyone wants what they can't have, so the less available someone is, the more attractive it makes them. It's just the way it is. For some reason too much of a good thing will always be, well too much of a good thing. That said, she needs to know your stance, and the sooner the better. Why not just tell her that while you really like her, things are moving too fast. Let her know that the constant contact is taking you out of your comfort zone. Tell her you look forward to spending time with her and you don't want to dilute it with too much telecommunication in-between. But keep in mind that if you're constantly unavailable or just too busy – she's likely to get fed up and find someone who is more accommodating.

### I'm confused, should I move in as soon as I spot her, or wait and assess the situation first?

There's no black and white answer I'm afraid. One school of thought says move in within five seconds of spotting her, any longer limits your chances. I do agree that too much over thinking can kill the moment, but it depends, if you see a 'closed' group of girls chattering like their life depends on it, you're not likely to get an encouraging response, unless you've got one hell of an opener. If you're confident enough and you can think on your feet – and handle any rejection, then yes, you should absolutely move in as soon as you spot her...

Personally however, I think the secret is to read the signs and assess the situation before you heading over. Look for the non-verbal cues. Is she swivelling her head and doing the 'lighthouse' as she checks out the talent in the room? Or is she locked in deep conversation? If so, you're better to bide your time before you approach.

**_I'm thinking of going speed dating. What's a great opening gambit?_**

If you've been paying attention – you would know that I'm big on avoiding the dreaded 'work' question, that's just going to drive the conversation right into oblivion. Use your common sense, look at the social context and use the stuff *you already have in common*. What's the season? Is it summer? That means holidays. Is it the weekend? That means fun. What about the area you're in? Is it worthy of note? Are there other cool places in the neighbourhood to check out afterwards? What about the venue, what makes it special? Good music, killer cocktails, Happy-Hour or great food? Research the place beforehand and use these things to find the common ground; from there it's just a matter of leading into shared interests.

## New Kid On The Kop

Now that you've done all your exercises, you should be crystal clear about your USP. The clearer you are, the more effectively you can sell yourself and the sooner she will be drawing blood from your freshly waxed back.

So, how do you size up when it comes to that dreaded Imaginary Clipboard? Do you feel like you've got it going on? Do you have the points on the board? And more importantly, do you feel bold and unshakeably confident about what you've got to offer? Hmmmm? Let's recap what we've gone through so far.

How do you present physically? What are your best features? Do you have a great smile and the personality to carry it? How would you describe your physical state? What about your sense of style, are you getting good feedback? In terms of personality, what is the overall impression you give off? Is it one of quiet confidence? Or are you a big alpha dog showboating all around the place? Are you in control of your life? Or do you get all bamboozled when you meet someone new? What makes you stand out from the crowd? Let's find out!

By now you should be feeling at the top of your game. But since no-one's perfect, there will be areas that need more work, so before you go crazy out there in dating land, why not sort out the weak areas and revisit them? To help get an idea of where you're at, grade yourself on a scale of 1 to 5 for each of the following:

### Physical

✓  General appearance (1 - 5)

✓  Image/Styling (1 - 5)

✓  Hygiene (1 - 5)

✓  Grooming (1 - 5)

✓  Physique (1 - 5)

✓  Fitness levels (1 - 5)

✓  Health  (1 - 5)


### Personality Characteristics

✓  Sense Of Humour (1 - 5)

✓  Strength of character (1 - 5)

✓  Trustfulness  (1 - 5)

✓  Reliability (1 - 5)

✓   Responsibility (1 - 5)

✓  Emotional Admin (1 - 5)


### Personal

✓  Psycho-Sexual Admin – are you on top of it? (1 – 5)

✓  Baggage – have you ditched the stuff that's holding you back? (1 – 5)

## Home Life

✓ General day to day organisation (1 - 5)

✓ Home – suitable for entertaining? (1 - 5)

## Social

✓ Interests/Activity Levels (1 - 5)

✓ Social Network (1 - 5)

✓ Female Friends (1 – 5)

✓ New interests (1 – 5)

✓ New challenges (1 – 5)

## Professional

✓ Are you happy in current career? (1 - 5)

✓ Have you looked into changing careers/jobs if you're unhappy? (1 – 5)

✓ Are challenging yourself out of the workplace? (1 – 5)

✓ Doing any extra curricular? (1 – 5)

✓ Learning anything new? (1 – 5)

✓ Have you tried Volunteering - for anything? (1 – 5)

**Scoreboard:**

Now tally up your score. The minimum number you're looking for is 80 points. Any less and you need to revisit the previous tasks and challenges. Otherwise apply to get your Flirting Personality accurately assessed by contacting: sue@flirtdiva.com

## Learning Outcomes:

✓ *HOMEWORK: practice, practice, practice on the person besides you, behind you, in-front of you – and your best friend's partner.*

✓ *MANNERS: Always say please and ask nicely - before tampering with someone you fancy.*

✓ *Keep your wits about you – and your sense of humour – you're going to need it!*

**Think about how far you think you've come since we started and write a few words to summarise (and give yourself a bonus 5 points for effort)**

*e.g.* Instead of shutting down in awkward situations I try to use humour and that's working for me. I'm surprised how easy it is to get a laugh when I'm just goofing around!

The areas that I'm still working on include body language and eye-contact which for some reason I still feel uncomfortable with.

I'm getting much better at the banter though. I've also made a massive effort to talk to strangers. It felt weird at first, but it's getting easier. I haven't met anyone special yet, but at least I know I can do it!

Now that you've come this far, don't lose your nerve, life's too short. If you see Missus Oh-My-Freakin-God you've got to go for it because the truth is, you most likely WON'T bump into her again. Strike while the iron's hot – lose the fear and flirt anyway.

With regular practice you'll be less likely to obsess about, *'How hot she is'*. That'll only turn you into Nervous Nigel, and we can't be having that!

Lastly it gives me great pleasure to say thanks for hanging in there guys. I know you love this dating advice stuff. You eat it up. You're responsive and diligent precisely because you appreciate that navigating the dating arena is hard work but that's what makes it FUN. You've got the ability to change your mindset to see how it's pretty funny, even when it's god-awful! It's all about confidence and being positive. Forget those first date nerves. *It's too many prunes you've got to worry about.*

So now, without any further ado, go forth and flirt.

*Thank-you and goodnight.*

## *Once Upon A Time.....*

She was working as a waitress in a cocktail bar when you met her, that much is true.

You picked her out and held her gaze and smiled at her.

All well and good....But then what happened?

Were you up for it? Prepared to chance it, and take that risk?

Or will you both miss out on a lifetime of potential happiness because you couldn't bring yourself to wander over.

What if you never find the nerve to say anything?

It's always easier to walk away but it's harder to stay. It takes guts to stay.

How important is it to stay safe and not take that risk?

Is at the expense of finding your possible true love?

Even if when you make an approach, they snigger and walk away.

Even if they ran away, or fled to the other side of the world

Even if you thought you didn't have a chance in hell.

Would you? Could you?

Will you...?

Also from Sue Ostler: *Get Over It; Get On With It; Relationships That Rock!* And *Flirt Diva:*

*"An inspiring guide to sexing up your life by the UK's top relationship sexpert"*
**Metro**

*"Sue Ostler's pro-level flirting lessons will help you to defy destiny!"*
**Cosmopolitan**

*"Sue Ostler really is the Queen of Love."*
**New Woman**

Lightning Source UK Ltd.
Milton Keynes UK
UKOW032315221111

182515UK00001B/5/P